Swaps

Swaps

by BARRY IRWIN

THOROUGHBRED
Legends®
No. 14

ECLIPSE
PRESS

Lexington, Kentucky

Library of Congress Control Number: 2001096883
ISBN 1-58150-071-8

Printed in The United States
First Edition: February 2002

a division of
The Blood-Horse, Inc.
PUBLISHERS SINCE 1916

To learn more about Swaps
and other classic Thoroughbreds, see:

www.thoroughbredlegends.com

SWAPS

CONTENTS

INTRODUCTION

Horse Of Many Myths

When horses reach legendary status, their stories are enhanced with each telling, and revisionist history clouds the events as they originally occurred.

The lines between actual and apocryphal episodes in the life of Swaps have been blurred more than usual, owing to iconoclastic connections who enjoyed tweaking the establishment by recasting history from the perspective of a cowboy just off the range and a Hollywood-style publicity engine that fed delicious stories to a seemingly insatiable media.

Case in point: the birth of Swaps on March 1, 1952.

Rex Cooper Ellsworth, the breeder and owner of Swaps, told a reporter at the height of his star's popularity that he knew from the ballet-like first step the newborn colt took to rise in the stall that Swaps was something special.

Another report placed the birth of Swaps outdoors in a puddle of rainwater where his dam foaled out of sight of the ranch staff.

Romantic followers of the sport prefer the Ellsworth version, because it supports a notion that the Arizona-born cowboy possessed a sixth sense about horses.

Most newborn foals struggle awkwardly with their initial steps. It would fit neatly into the legend of Swaps if his lissome manner in rising to his feet really had struck lifelong horseman Ellsworth as unusually graceful, because it was the effortless motion of Swaps' stride that later would become his hallmark on the racetrack.

Adding another layer to the rich patina that would imbue Swaps with an almost mythical status is the tale of the gleaming chestnut colt standing in front of the Churchill Downs racing office while tied to a hitching post, as trainer Mesach "Mish" Tenney went inside to fetch the mail.

Had Tenney really ridden the colt that would soon win the Kentucky Derby from his barn to the office to get the mail? Some say yes; some say no.

Whether such accounts occurred, were made up, or were simply allowed to go without challenge, one thing

is certain — they served to embellish the legend of
Swaps.

Fueling the tales of Swaps was the chasm between
the colt's cowboy connections and the bluebloods
always identified with the Sport of Kings. Members of
the press loved to snub the nose of a swell when an
opportunity presented itself. And in Ellsworth and
Tenney the media had a pair of heroes all too willing to
poke fun at practices long held sacrosanct by those
who developed and nurtured the Turf sport.

"With Tenney or Ellsworth, it's not whether it happened or not; the operative thing was that you believe
it could have happened," said former Ellsworth business partner Dr. Arnold G. Pessin.

Swaps, as a mature horse, looked the part of patri-
cian, and he had the blood to back it up. His profile
exhibited a cameo quality. He was tall and had a regal
bearing. He moved with an athleticism that belied his
height (16.2 hands) and size (1,200 pounds).

He was from the first crop of Khaled, a son of Lord
Derby's Hyperion, whom Ellsworth bought from the
Aga Khan. Swaps' dam, Iron Reward, who was sired by
the elegant import Beau Pere, descended from a family

that produced a steady stream of tough, classy runners in America. Two years after Swaps won the Kentucky Derby, his grandam would also be represented by a Kentucky Derby winner in Calumet Farm's Iron Liege.

Yet, despite Swaps' aristocratic background and his handlers' recognition that he was born special, the California colt was treated in a singularly plebian fashion that was the norm for the Ellsworth-Tenney operation.

Because of this unorthodox treatment, the prince who would be king became the subject of much ink in the press, airtime on the radio, and star billing on the television as he climbed to the top of the racing game.

In one of the enduring ironies of the Turf, a miscast Swaps was characterized as a rough-hewn cayuse handled by a couple of cheapskate cowpunchers from the sun-baked Arizona desert and juxtaposed with Nashua, a contemporary stylized as a regally blooded Kentucky-bred equine icon conditioned by Establishment trainer James "Sunny Jim" Fitzsimmons and owned by The Jockey Club stalwart William Woodward Jr. of Belair Stud.

In a Hollywood movie, Gary Cooper would have played Ellsworth, Alan Ladd would have been Tenney, and Robert Taylor would have been Woodward. Swaps' double would have been rented from a Burbank riding stable, and a sleek black Arab on loan from the famed Kellogg Ranch would have portrayed Nashua.

Blacklisted writer Dalton Trumbo's screenplay would have been directed by noted liberal Marty Ritt, because all of the elements of a blockbuster class struggle were present — rich vs. poor, establishment vs. outsider, East vs. West, urban vs. rural, sophisticate vs. common man, sportsmanship vs. commerce, royalty vs. bourgeoisie, and purist vs. unorthodox iconoclast.

At a time when a nation's sensibilities had been shaped by the beginning of the Cold War in a post-McCarthy era, the ingredients that went into the Swaps-Nashua rivalry were the stuff of dreams for those who publicized the Turf sport.

The trainers of both horses also were at opposite ends of the spectrum, as Fitzsimmons was nearly as old as the modern era of the sport and relied on traditional methods to ready his stock, whereas Tenney had some newfangled cowpoke ideas based on life on the range.

Even the riders of the two colts were different. Swaps was partnered by shy Willie Shoemaker, a miniature upstart who sat perched atop the withers of a horse with perfect balance and used finesse and soft hands to communicate with his mounts, while Nashua was ridden by the brash Eddie Arcaro, a powerful reinsman who used his strength and savvy to get the most out of his mounts.

It didn't matter that precious little truth lay in pegging Swaps as a cattle pony. The Swaps-Nashua debate made for the best rivalry since the West's Seabiscuit and the East's War Admiral. The media saw to it that troops on both sides of the country were properly polarized and armed with ammunition for what would become a lifelong battle over supremacy between the two camps.

The paths of Swaps and Nashua crossed in such a way that these two marvelous Thoroughbreds would be inseparably linked for all time.

The clash of horses and wills between Ellsworth-Tenney and Woodward was unique at the time but would prove a harbinger for the direction in which horse racing was headed.

The Westerner represented one of a new breed of Thoroughbred owner — the entrepreneur. With borrowed money, he gambled that he could play the game better than anybody else. He treated racing as a business.

The Easterner represented the traditional owner whose racing stable was stocked with horses bred by him and his family over generations. He relied on resources handed down from one generation to the next. He treated racing as a sport.

This changing of the guard, in which burgeoning individual forces of commercialism would challenge the established principles of forming a racing dynasty, was in its infancy in the mid-1950s.

Although Ellsworth was a representative of a new trend, he was more a one-of-a-kind individual who shook the very foundations of the sport in achieving unprecedented success by employing methods that completely went against the grain of standards long accepted as valid.

In many ways, Swaps was the embodiment of the Ellsworth method of breeding and racing a Thoroughbred.

Swaps early on gave this experienced horseman a glimpse of an ease of movement that would later allow

him to perform gracefully under the most intense competitive pressures the Turf had to offer. In the process, the red colt put on a display of sheer speed that kindled the imaginations of racing fans like no other runner since Man o' War.

Barry Irwin
Versailles, Kentucky 2001

CHAPTER 1

An Eye For A Horse

R ex Cooper Ellsworth trusted his judgment in horses enough to stake his career on it. Born in 1907 to a devout Mormon family, Ellsworth grew up on a cattle ranch his father ran north of Tucson in southeastern Arizona near the small town of Safford. The early settlers in the Gila River Valley lived a wild and rugged lifestyle, as the neighboring Apache Indians had a proactive leader in Geronimo.

Ellsworth and his brothers learned early how to ride and care for horses. At eight years of age, Ellsworth undertook tasks that required responsibility, and at seventeen, his father, William, put him in charge of a thousand head of cattle.

The practical knowledge Ellsworth gleaned from having to rely on a horse to run cattle and transport him through the severe swings of climate and terrain in the Gila River Valley provided a solid foundation.

Stoic, introspective, and analytical, Ellsworth used these qualities to become self-sufficient in managing a horse operation on a ranch or a training stable.

He developed practical skills, such as shoeing a horse, making a saddle, and repairing tack, that later allowed him to set up and oversee an entire equine operation.

As an urban teenager would learn to tear apart and rebuild a hot rod, so Ellsworth learned how to pick apart a horse. His deeply analytical mind took him a step further. He used the parched sands, craggy canyons, and stony riverbanks of the Arizona desert as his own laboratory to test, through trial and error, every possible part of a horse's make-up, to find out what worked and what was possible on horseback.

In 1956, when Swaps was breaking track record after track record, Ellsworth estimated that he had spent more than half of his life in a saddle.

"During that long a time, you learn what you are riding and why and where and a great deal about it," he said. "In riding the country and under the conditions we rode, I had to take care of myself and try to figure out the best horses to do this with. Eventually, I think I learned something about the conformation of a horse."

More than one acquaintance of Ellsworth echoed the sentiments of Joe Estes, editor of *The Blood-Horse*. Estes wrote, after Swaps had won the Kentucky Derby, "I don't know anybody whose judgment of a horse is more to be trusted than Rex Ellsworth's."

Ellsworth once said, "I shod my first mare when I was eight years old. No one has ever shod a horse for me since." He said, "It's all done from experience shoeing my own horses, then getting on and riding them and putting them through it."

Asked once how he felt about a front leg that buckles over slightly at the knee as opposed to a knee that is concave (calf knee), Ellsworth answered: "Rather have one than a calf knee by two hundred percent. I can truthfully say that I've never walked home in my life because my mount was buck kneed, but the reverse is true of calf knees.

"A horse cannot stand up as a saddle horse if he has calf knees and isn't likely to as a racehorse. I've walked afoot behind many a herd of cattle leading a tired, calf-kneed horse."

Strong opinions based on his personal experience stood Ellsworth in good stead when he decided to invest in horses at the height of the Great Depression. Making money with cattle had become difficult. Ellsworth wanted to try his luck breeding and racing horses. He got the bug riding impromptu races on the ranch before he was ten and later developed a passion for the sport by reading magazines published in Kentucky.

Ellsworth's only experience with racing stock had come with Quarter Horses in the bushes of the Southwest. But he had thought a lot about buying some Thoroughbreds.

"You know what I'm gonna do when I get the first five hundred dollars I don't know what to do with?" Ellsworth told his bride, Nola. "Well, I'm gonna give $250 to you, and I'm gonna take $250, go to Kentucky, and buy a racehorse."

His father was against it. "Nola, are you gonna let Rex go to Kentucky and buy a horse?" he asked.

"Yes," said Mrs. Ellsworth.

"You are!" William Ellsworth exclaimed.

"Yes," repeated Nola.

"Well, how come?" the father asked.

"Look, I'm married to him, and I don't have to worry about anything except that Rex loves horses. He got that from you. And I'm going along with it."

In 1933 Ellsworth rented a Ford truck, drove to Kentucky, and arrived ten minutes before an auction at the Lexington Sales Paddocks on Paris Pike. From a seventy-five-dollar monthly salary he earned as his father's foreman, Ellsworth had $625 in savings. He spent six hundred dollars for six mares and two weanlings, leaving him a bankroll of twenty-five dollars, which he used to keep the claptrap truck roadworthy on the long trip back to Safford.

Soaked by rain and baked by the sun because the elements had eaten the roof off the truck, the eight horses arrived in a state of disarray at the Ellsworth Ranch in Arizona. A Mormon, William Ellsworth disapproved of his son's participating in racing because gambling was forbidden in his religion. Rex explained that he did not gamble, and if others were foolish enough to bet on horses, their folly should not be held against him.

A year later Ellsworth returned to the Bluegrass in search of a Thoroughbred stallion he could breed to Quarter Horse mares. He bought Silver Cord, even though the horse had a breathing problem, reasoning it was not a heritable trait.

The ragtag first draft of six mares and the brilliant agent of precocity, Silver Cord, provided Ellsworth with winners and an increased bankroll. "Silver Cord and his get moved them (the Ellsworths) from quarter racing to Hollywood Park," wrote Estes in *The Blood-Horse*.

One of the six original mares bought for one hundred dollars by Ellsworth was Legotal, a seventeen-year-old that became blind. Her first foal for Ellsworth was Arigotal, who would sire Ellsworth's speedy Roman In, a horse that in 1950 beat Citation at Golden Gate Fields while equaling the world record of 1:08 2/5 for six furlongs.

Ellsworth stood Silver Cord in New Mexico, raised his foals in Arizona, and raced the best ones in California. By the mid-1940s Ellsworth was raising California-bred foals at his ranch in Ontario.

Invariably cash poor and cattle rich, Ellsworth had to

be creative to build up and improve his Thoroughbred holdings.

Ellsworth did a lot of business with ex-cowboy Ray Bell, one of the most successful bloodstock agents of the era and a Thoroughbred adviser to movie mogul Louis B. Mayer. "Rex went out to Mayer's place one day and examined the stallions," recalled Bell's son, Thomas R. Bell. "He phoned Dad and said, 'I'll take ten breedings to that sorrel horse — he meant Alibhai — and ten to that Beau Pere. I don't have any cash, but I'll trade him some cattle.'

"Well, Mayer sent his farm manager to check out Rex's cattle, and they made a deal. Shortly afterwards, the price of cattle about doubled, and Mayer made a killing."

Ellsworth was able to make significant strides in shaping his broodmare band. "You'll notice that anyone building up a good herd of cattle, sheep, hogs, or any other livestock does a lot of culling before he's successful," he said. "The man that does the most culling is the man who winds up with the best herd."

The strength of Ellsworth's broodmare band at the close of the 1940s, in the days immediately before he would dominate racing in North America, was in well-conformed individuals.

"As everyone knows, I chose conformation as the basis of selection of my breeding stock in preference to pedigree or performance, because that's what I could afford," he explained in a speech on the subject of conformation delivered to his peers in 1956 at a meeting of the California Thoroughbred Breeders' Association.

"Conformation is so often ignored that it is the cheapest of all measures. It isn't in books or statistics readily available to anyone who can read. To me, it wouldn't make any difference, though, how well bred a horse was, anyone would be foolish to take a chance on him if he didn't come up to their specifications or standards of conformation. If he does and has solid breeding, he's going to be all right."

Conformation to Ellsworth became a lifelong obsession and subject of considerable study.

"When I first worked for him at the ranch in 1954 when they had moved to Chino, I would go out on rounds with Rex," recalled stable veterinarian Jock Jocoy. "Everybody had to be up before sun break.

"Rex would stand there and look at a yearling or a two-year-old. He wouldn't say a word for the longest time. Sometimes thirty minutes would go by. Then he would make one of those short cowboy comments of his to me. But it really wasn't to me, if you know what I mean. It was just a comment made out loud.

"He would say something about the length of the horse or some such comment and say how good a horse it was going to be. Rex Ellsworth's greatest enjoyment, his biggest thrill, was to study a horse and figure out what it was going to be able to do.

"And then he would go back four generations in the pedigree and tell me about all of its ancestors and how this one looked like that one. It was his passion. Sometimes we would be standing there until 9:30 in the morning, and I'd finally say something like, 'Hey, isn't it time for breakfast?' "

Tales of Ellsworth standing in a stall for an hour at a time examining a single horse are numerous. Joe Estes, on a European trip with Ellsworth, wrote, "I also learned something about Rex Ellsworth's judgment of a horse." Estes was with him in Italy when Ellsworth "picked out a future champion after sunset in a stall so dark I could see only the blurred outline of a horse."

After World War II, Ellsworth was ready to take the next step in developing his Thoroughbred operation — he was ready to buy his first world-class stallion.

CHAPTER 2

Stallion Shopping

R ex Ellsworth had reached a financial position in which he felt able to buy a stallion that not only looked the part, but had the blood to match. He wanted to buy a stallion that would do justice to his improving band of broodmares. He was ready to make the ultimate selection.

"I wanted a stallion, and I wanted a good one," Ellsworth said. "In this country, I know that everybody who has a good horse keeps him, and there's little chance of buying a really top stallion prospect."

A man of considerable intellect, Ellsworth pored over books and magazines as he refined and narrowed his choices. A photograph of The Tetrarch riveted his attention. Ellsworth considered the so-called "Spotted Wonder" to have ideal conformation. He wanted to find one like him in the British Isles.

The horse Ellsworth finally settled on was Nasrullah, a colt of the finest quality, conformation, and bloodlines, whose racing career had been compromised by an unruly temperament.

Nasrullah and The Tetrarch both possessed a shape that would soon come to typify what is now called a (D. Wayne) "Lukas horse." They both had powerful hips and looked coiled and ready to spring into action while standing still.

On behalf of Ellsworth, Ray Bell in the late summer of 1946 asked English trainer Harry "The Head Waiter" Wragg to see whether a deal could be struck to buy Nasrullah, whom the Aga Khan had sold during World War II to Irish horseman Joe McGrath for $76,000. Nasrullah's first foals were yearlings at the time.

The Blood-Horse editor Joe Estes, who first met Ellsworth when the then twenty-seven-year-old Arizonan had come to the Bluegrass and bought Silver Cord, played a role in the search for a stallion. "Sometime in September, 1946," wrote Estes, "Rex telephoned me and said 'I want you to go to Europe with me next week.'

"I couldn't go to Europe — too busy, didn't have a birth certificate anyway. But somehow I went, with

Rex and his delightful brother, Heber, a personification of the cow-punching Southwest."

Ellsworth failed to buy Nasrullah. He was told the horse was not for sale. Later, Ellsworth sensed McGrath did not think the cowboy could afford Nasrullah. He told a reporter, years later, that if he had been more experienced, he would have been able to make a deal.

(A while later, the savvy internationalist A.B. "Bull" Hancock Jr. formed a syndicate to acquire and stand Nasrullah at his famed Claiborne Farm in Paris, Kentucky, where the horse became one of the most important sires of the twentieth century, his offspring including Nashua, who would become the nemesis of Swaps.)

When the Nasrullah transaction died, Ellsworth briefly shifted his focus to Gulf Stream, a son of leading sire Hyperion owned by Lord Derby. The colt had been unbeaten at two and won the Eclipse Stakes at three. The price was $100,000.

"Harry Wragg introduced him to Aly Khan," said Tommy Bell, "and Rex and the prince hit it off. Two total opposites, yet they got on really well with each other."

Aly Khan, a shrewd vendor of horseflesh, tried to

interest Ellsworth in Khaled. This son of Hyperion had been unbeaten at two, during which time he won the Middle Park Stakes. He disappointed at three when he had been unable to take advantage of the considerable stamina in his pedigree.

Ellsworth loved everything about Khaled but had been puzzled why the colt did not stay the longer distances required of a classic-winning three-year-old. The prince persuaded Ellsworth to visit the stallion prospect in Ireland at Onngar Stud, where the staff had been told to restrict Khaled's activity to walking.

When the handler was reluctant to take Khaled out of his stall, Ellsworth punched the horse in the belly. A groan, typical of a horse with a chronic breathing problem, told Ellsworth all he needed to know. He had Khaled turned out in a pasture and when the elegant bay horse swung into motion, the full-blown nature of the horse's breathing ailment was out in the open. Khaled was a "roarer," a condition in which a horse makes a raspy breathing sound due to partial paralysis of the larynx.

Instead of being put off by the breathing ailment, Ellsworth viewed the situation as positive because it showed him that Khaled's inability to stay was attributable to an acquired condition.

With his first stallion acquisition in Silver Cord, Ellsworth had already enjoyed considerable success buying a "roarer." Ellsworth considered the ailment to be a result of external forces and not a weakness passed on in the genes.

"In those days, Aly was always in need of money," said Bell. "He liked to bet and ran with a fast crowd. The old Aga had him on some kind of a retainer, but Aly always ran short of cash. One way he could make some money was to sell his father's horses."

Prince Aly Khan successfully shifted Ellsworth's interest away from Gulf Stream and onto Khaled.

"Rex made his deal directly with the prince," Bell said. "The price was $160,000. Harry told Rex he could go to the Aga and get Khaled for less. Harry thought the prince was making something for himself. But Rex said that he had made a deal and he would stick by it."

Ellsworth did not have all of the money required and arranged to borrow the difference from a bank back home. It is a measure of how much Ellsworth wanted Khaled that he agreed to buy him under a stip-

ulation that called for the horse to stand on behalf of the seller for the 1947 breeding season in Ireland. Aly Khan had already booked mares for Khaled's initial season, and he did not want to go back on his word with Irish breeders.

Khaled fit Ellsworth's criteria. He was bred in the purple. (His broodmare sire was even a son of Ellsworth's much-admired The Tetrarch.) He demonstrated high-class form on the racecourse. (He ranked among the top on the English Free Handicap at two.) He was conformed well enough to pass his new owner's high standards.

As an experiment to satisfy himself that even in a diminished state Khaled would be able to show form over a route of ground, Ellsworth placed the son of Hyperion back in training. He reasoned that the lighter, desert-like air in Southern California, as opposed to the heavier, more humid air in England, would make it easier for Khaled to breathe under the stress of racing.

Whether the results of Khaled's brief reappearance under silks in California satisfied Ellsworth is debatable. Following a season at stud in Ireland, Khaled ran three times in January at Santa Anita, winning at one and one-sixteenth miles on dirt in his best effort. He was brought back at the end of the 1948 season in December and finished last on a sloppy track.

To everyone but Ellsworth, Khaled hardly looked a gilt-edged investment opportunity at the start of the 1949 breeding season. Because he was fast early at two and disappointed at three, he looked like a flash in the pan that did not train on. His brief stint racing on dirt at Santa Anita did little to encourage local breeders to flock to him.

On the other hand, he had shown enough brilliance at two to win an important fixture in the Middle Park Stakes. His pedigree, although foreign, was not unfamiliar to the more astute breeders in California, who recognized its quality.

His sire, Hyperion, was a magical name worldwide in Thoroughbred breeding. The son of Triple Crown winner Gainsborough had won the Epsom Derby (officially by four lengths, but eyewitnesses said it was closer to ten) in record time and then became the premier sire of his time standing for Lord Derby in England.

A diminutive chestnut with four white socks, nineteen-year-old Hyperion in 1949 was already well on

his way in establishing branches of his line in America through his sons Heliopolis (sire of Olympia and Summer Tan) and Alibhai (sire of Your Host and Traffic Judge).

Eclair, the dam of Khaled, was named by Ellsworth as the best-looking horse he saw on his trip to Britain.

Khaled from matings to twenty mares in his initial Irish season at stud came up with nine foals, five of them winners, two of which showed a bit of class, and none of which made horsemen in Ireland bemoan his departure to the States.

Entering stud at Ellsworth's ranch in Ontario, Khaled initially stood for a fee of $1,500. His first two crops of thirty-seven and forty-seven foals were by far the largest for a major stallion in North America.

Among those bred to Khaled in his second season was Iron Reward, a mare Ellsworth had bought from W.W. "Tiny" Naylor, a large man with a big appetite for horses whose business enterprises included a well-known family restaurant chain in Southern California named Tiny Naylor's.

A daughter of Beau Pere, Iron Reward was the first produce of a storied mare in Iron Maiden.

"I saw Iron Maiden win one of her first races," Naylor said, "and her time was so good that I got in touch with L.B. Mayer's office and bought her right away for $7,500."

Iron Maiden, racing at two and three, won four races from nineteen starts. Naylor bred her at four to the 17.1-hand Beau Pere. She had a difficult breach birth that resulted in a healthy filly but required several stitches. Naylor dumped the mare on Ellwood B. "Pie Man" Johnston, a friend and business partner in the flagship Tiny Naylor's, which became a Hollywood landmark on the corner of Sunset and La Brea.

Johnston, a sawed-off dynamo of a man, was just figuring out a sport he would later master as the owner of Old English Rancho, a California nursery that led all breeders of stakes winners in 1972 and developed Fleet Nasrullah before the horse was syndicated by Leslie B. Combs II and John W. Hanes to stand at Spendthrift Farm in Kentucky.

"Pie Man" Johnston thought Iron Maiden looked very sound, so he put her back in training at six. The daughter of War Admiral thrived. The remarkable iron-made mare started an additional forty-two times

at six and seven, ending her racing career with twelve wins. Among them was the 1947 Del Mar Handicap at the direct expense of a tough male handicapper in Be Fearless, leading her to become the fourth consecutive stakes-winning female in her family.

Ellsworth bought Iron Reward, the first foal of Iron Maiden, in 1947 as a yearling in a three-horse package from breeder Naylor. Ellsworth raced Iron Reward eight times; her best finish was a fourth, and she earned only $425 in her career. Weak ankles precipitated her retirement.

Iron Reward had shown some speed, but more important she had a very good pedigree. Aside from her family, which boasted four consecutive stakes-winning dams, her sire, Beau Pere, had become a sensation at stud for Mayer.

Stoutly bred and reasonably successful as a handicapper in England, the Son-in-Law horse realized a paltry one hundred guineas at the 1933 Newmarket December Sales as a six-year-old and was sent to New Zealand, where he proved an instant success and led the sire list in Australia three times.

Mayer purchased Beau Pere just prior to the

33

Japanese attack on Pearl Harbor and brought him to California, where the stallion's success continued. Beau Pere sired Mayer's enormously successful California distaffer Honeymoon. A year before purchasing Iron Reward, Ellsworth had won his first stakes race as an owner when his Beau Pere filly U Time took the Hollywood Lassie Stakes.

Prior to mating Iron Reward to Khaled, both were unknown quantities. This would change dramatically in the ensuing years. The first mating between the pair produced Track Medal, who would go on to become Broodmare of the Year for Greentree Stud in 1962.

Iron Maiden was sold in 1948 by Johnston, through Henry Knight, to Calumet Farm, in whose silks her son Iron Liege would win the 1957 Kentucky Derby over Gallant Man, Bold Ruler, and Round Table.

Khaled with his second crop, which raced the year Swaps was born, sired a sensational twenty-six winners at two, one short of the American record set by Star Shoot in 1916.

Khaled would become the most successful California sire of the modern era, finishing second on the General Sire list to Nasrullah in 1956 and siring

sixty-one stakes winners, among them A Glitter (Coaching Club American Oaks), Terrang (Santa Anita Handicap), Correspondent (Blue Grass Stakes), Corn Off the Cob (Arlington Classic), Going Abroad (Hawthorne Gold Cup), Light Talk (Arkansas Derby), Linmold (Santa Anita Handicap), Fleet Khal (Vanity Handicap), Take Over (Washington Park Handicap), Physician (Santa Anita Handicap), and Annie-Lu-San (Vanity Handicap).

It was the second union between Khaled and Iron Reward that would give Ellsworth the *beau ideal* he had spent a lifetime striving to create: Swaps.

SWAPS

CHAPTER 3

Perfect Partners

Mesach Adams Tenney lived in a house on the Ellsworth Ranch. Each morning in the spring of 1954, he would leave before five o'clock to take the hour-long drive to Santa Anita or Hollywood Park. When he got home, Tenney could count on Ellsworth asking him about Swaps.

Most times Tenney would tell the boss that the big red colt by Khaled "wasn't showing much interest."

"Ellsworth was the king of the operation," said Dr. Jock Jocoy, whose second professional stint after graduating from veterinary school was at the Ellsworth Ranch in 1954. Ellsworth ran the ranch, planned the matings, raised the foals, shod the stock, and developed a scientific feeding program. But when the young horses were sent to the track, Tenney was in charge.

Called Mish by his friends and Mesach or Mischa by

his family, Tenney had Ellsworth's complete trust. They were born a day apart, the elder Ellsworth in Arizona and Tenney in Mexico. The Tenney family repatriated to Safford prior to World War I, and the parents went to work for the Ellsworths as ranch hands at the spread in Arizona. Tenney and Ellsworth had been inseparable since the age of eight, sharing a love of horses and rodeo.

When school was dismissed on Friday afternoons, Tenney and Ellsworth would disappear on horseback and, unless somebody roped them into going to Sunday school, would not be seen again until the dinner bell rang on Sunday evening.

As young teenagers, the tall, reed-thin Ellsworth and the short, wiry Tenney began to win money calf roping at local rodeos and used the prize money to upgrade their mounts.

Tenney and Ellsworth developed their skills as horsemen so that when they grew up both could do anything and everything with a horse, and each was fully capable of doing the other's job. But the marriage of Tenney and Ellsworth flourished because each gravitated toward the specialty he was most passionate about.

Ellsworth fixated on creating a particular type of racehorse, raising it in a controlled environment of his own design, and feeding it the best ingredients the earth had to offer. Tenney reveled in conditioning an athlete to realize its ultimate potential in competition.

Ellsworth designed the ranch in Chino after a cattle operation. Built for functionality and not for show, the simplistic layout allowed a single cowboy to be able to load an entire van of horses by himself, as all of the aisles and pens connected to a chute.

Ellsworth spent $250,000 to have a ninety-foot-high electric feed mill built, then scoured the world in search of the finest feed and micronutrients to produce pellets that Jocoy described as the equine equivalent of the nutritional supplements used by today's elite human athletes. A kelp imported from Norway, as an example, contained more than sixty trace minerals and vitamins.

Tenney, although short in stature, had been a high-school star in track and field, taking the 100- and 220-yard dashes, along with the broad jump, in the Arizona Eastern Division Championship meet at Safford. No mindless jock, Tenney was deeply analytical, and he

was able to bring his experiences in athletic conditioning to the shed row when he began training horses for Ellsworth.

"There was such a mystique about him," Jocoy said of Mesach Tenney. "He led such an exemplary life, he set himself apart. That's the reason why he went to winning all the big races.

"Tenney didn't go to the kitchen, he didn't sit and drink coffee with everybody. After he did his work around the barn and shod or trimmed a horse or two, he would go right to his tack room, close his door, read his Bible, and go right to sleep.

"He slept at home at night with his family. Left the house every morning at precisely five o'clock. Was never late to the barn one day in his life. The only luxury he allowed himself was an Oldsmobile. Lord he loved that Olds. Mish was meticulous about every detail in his life and that Olds was a case in point. He had it shining like all get out."

Tenney never looked or acted like anything but what he was — a rock hard cowboy. He grew up on a cattle ranch and ate lean red beef three times a day. He shod at least one horse in his barn every day, possessed a back as hard as river rock, and was his own man.

"Mish was no kowtow to Rex," said Jocoy, "and Rex didn't treat him that way, either."

The lifelong friends uniquely complemented each other. The cowboys' extraordinary success by means of unorthodox methods in the next decade dominated conversations among horsemen from the Fair Grounds to the Curragh and created a mystique about Tenney and Ellsworth.

"They were men, real men," said Jocoy. "They could hold their own in any company. They never drank or swore or touched a cigarette. Their word was their bond, and they had a work ethic one does not see anymore. They were strong minded and believed in themselves and each other."

Tenney married his bride, Sylvia, the morning of January 29, 1935, and in the afternoon saddled his first Thoroughbred winner at a recognized track, when he sent out the broken-winded eight-year-old Silver Cord to score at Phoenix.

A decade later Tenney saddled his first horse to win a stakes. Yet another decade later he saddled the Horse of the Year in Swaps.

The burnished golden chestnut with the faraway look in his eyes did not arrive on earth as a fully realized equine angel. He came into the world as wild as any other colt.

In learning the "Arizona Method" from Mesach Tenney, Swaps began to develop a mental well being, allowing his physical gifts to blossom to their fullest.

"We keep our horses content because we always give them a clear, understandable signal of everything we want them to do. When there's nothing to do, we give them their head," explained the trainer.

"Horses learn by experience what man requires of them and, in gaining that experience, I've never seen anyone improve on what I call the 'Arizona Method.' A horse is treated as a horse, with affection, to be sure, but without what Arizonans consider to be a lot of nonsense." Still, Swaps did not strike his trainer as Horse of the Year material before his first race. "Fact is, he was a little on the lazy side far as work went as a two-year-old," Tenney said.

Art Sherman, later a successful trainer in San Francisco, was a seventeen-year-old exercise rider for Tenney in 1954. He remembered Swaps as "an awful green, big, raw-boned colt who was still growing when he came to the track."

Swaps made his racing debut May 20, 1954, at Hollywood Park, sent off as the sixth choice among eleven at odds of more than 12-1. He scored by three lengths. He "ran in" on Tenney and Ellsworth, meaning that he surprised them by winning. He was sharp early, pressing the pace of Irish Cheer, took over before the final furlong, and drew off to score "handily" in :58 2/5 for five furlongs. The beaten favorite was the Nasrullah colt Blue Ruler, who would develop into a high-class colt that would be heard from later.

Swaps had been among the last draft of horses broken at Ellsworth's Ontario ranch before operations were moved to Chino. "The way we looked at it, Swaps had no more, no less chance than the others," Tenney said later.

For such a big colt, Swaps had reached the races early, a fairly routine matter for a son of Khaled, who had become something of a sensation as a sire of precocious juveniles. Two weeks after his debut victory, Swaps returned again over five furlongs for the Westchester Stakes at Hollywood Park.

Regular stable rider John Burton was up again, and he had fourth-choice Swaps fifth of seven turning for home, but only about three and a half lengths from the lead. Swaps still had only two runners beat a furlong from home, and he fell an additional length behind. In the last eighth of a mile Swaps made up all but two and a quarter lengths of the deficit to finish "gamely" for third.

"Swaps was fast all right," Tenney said, "but he had courage, too. That's something you find out as you go along. Swaps is game. He'll struggle when you ask him to."

Tenney decided to bring Swaps back a week later for the June Juvenile Stakes. The big colt, in a rare show of ornery behavior, gave Tenney fits on the afternoon of the race when the trainer attempted to fit him with new racing plates. Tenney feared for a time he would have to scratch the chestnut.

Favored for the five-furlong dash at odds of 1-2 was Trentonian, who had finished second as the odds-on choice in the Westchester Stakes won by Black Hoe. The Calumet Farm colorbearer had been foaled by Swaps' remarkable grandam Iron Maiden.

Sent away under Burton as the 9-2 second choice among seven, Swaps raced in mid-pack down the backstretch, moved up to third within two lengths of the lead turning for home, and took command before reaching the final furlong.

Burton got after the big colt in the last eighth of a mile and Swaps responded, drawing off to win by two and a half lengths in :58 2/5 over Trentonian, who "collided" with long shot Noir at the top of the lane and lost his best chance in the short dash.

Twelve days later, Swaps was back for more in the Haggin Stakes, also at five furlongs. Coupled in the wagering with Bequeath, Swaps went off at odds of more than 6-1, the entry being the fourth choice in a field comprising eight betting interests.

Mr. Sullivan, part of an entry held at odds of more than 10-1, and favored Black Hoe, the Westchester winner, ran one-two all the way, with pacesetter Mr. Sullivan prevailing by a half-length under Bill Shoemaker.

John Burton had Swaps eighth of ten early in the race. The colt made up considerable ground to reach a contending position into the stretch and then was forced to ease out of close quarters when boxed in nearing the furlong pole. Swaps regenerated his bid and finished a good third, beaten two lengths.

Swaps ran his only bad race at two in the July 8 Charles S. Howard Stakes at five and a half furlongs. Odds-on choice Colonel Mack beat Mr. Sullivan and Black Hoe in 1:04 4/5. Sent off as the last choice at odds of nearly 10-1 among six runners in a field with five betting interests, Swaps beat only stablemate Bequeath, *Daily Racing Form*'s chart noting he "showed nothing."

The Khaled colt showed something back at the barn, however: a thermometer revealed his temperature to be 105 degrees. Tenney sent the hard-used two-year-old back to the Ellsworth Ranch after five races in forty-nine days.

Kentucky Bound

S waps was ready to begin his Classic campaign when Santa Anita opened the day after Christmas, a week before the start of the 1955 season. The penny had dropped, and Swaps, with five races under his girth, had the mindset of a racehorse when he stripped for his comeback on the penultimate day of 1954.

An open allowance sprint for two-year-olds lured a dozen horses; four — Colonel Mack (115 pounds), Beau Busher (114), Swaps (111), and Battle Dance (108) — would be weighted on the Experimental Free Handicap, a hypothetical ranking of the previous season's best youngsters.

Swaps "forced the pace in hand," put away Battle Dance inside the eighth pole, then "stalled off" Beau Busher to win by a nose as the 5-1 third choice. He ran six furlongs in 1:10, four-fifths of a second slower than the older filly Miz Clementine required a race later behind similar fractions.

Swaps was ridden for the first time by Bill Shoemaker, who was given the assignment after John Burton, a Mormon, left racing to fulfill a religious commitment. Tenney and Ellsworth, both devoutly religious Mormons, did not easily place trust in those outside of their faith.

Both owner and trainer, however, came to realize that if they wanted to reach the top rung of the racing game, they would need to ride better jockeys. When Burton left for his mission for the church, an opportunity arose to upgrade their outfit.

"[Jockey] Eddie Arcaro was on a train from Maryland up to New York that fall and was sitting next to Rex Ellsworth," Shoemaker said. "Rex was telling him about Swaps, how good he was, and how anybody could ride him. Arcaro said 'If you can get a kid named Shoemaker, you better take him, because he is the best rider out there.' Rex decided to take his advice."

Swaps first served notice he would be a force in his initial start at three, when he made an eye-catching move around the turn in the January 19 San Vicente Stakes at seven furlongs.

Sent away in an entry at 9-2 odds in an eight-horse

field, in which California-bred Guerrero was a slight 9-5 favorite over 2-1 Trentonian, Swaps was under a good tug from Shoemaker down the backstretch.

When Shoemaker unloosened his grip, Swaps moved with a startling rush, looping his field on the turn to reach pacesetting Guerrero at the head of the lane. He quickly opened up a considerable margin.

The image of the diminutive Shoemaker crossing the wire three and a half lengths to the good on the statuesque Swaps is most memorable. He is standing tall in the saddle, his knees virtually locked, while his little left hand gently fingers a bit of rein, and his right hand holds his whip at an odd angle as if it were a ballast. Shoemaker, perched precariously atop the speeding Swaps, looks as if he is riding a runaway red locomotive.

The *Daily Racing Form* noted Swaps "was taken in hand through the final sixteenth to appear much the best." Final time on a muddy strip was 1:24. Trentonian ran second; Jean's Joe, third; and Guerrero, fourth.

Swaps came out of the San Vicente with a foot ailment.

"He developed an infection in his right fore foot," Tenney said of the ailment beneath the sole. "It came from a piece of dirt working up in a crack."

The foot problem would haunt Swaps and his connections for the remainder of his career.

Tenney wanted to run the colt back a week later in the California Breeders' Champion Stakes. This option was lost when Ellsworth learned that the nomination form he dropped into a country mailbox on a Saturday had not been picked up until Monday and the late postmark had cost his colt a chance to race. The infected foot probably would have prevented Swaps from starting anyway.

The trainer had exactly a month to prepare Swaps for the Santa Anita Derby. Swaps had never run around two turns, and the Derby was run over a mile and one-eighth. Tenney went to work healing and protecting the foot and making a schedule he hoped would deliver a fit colt for the February 19 Santa Anita Derby.

Using a lanolin-based ointment containing natural medicine that he had developed when riding horses on the cattle range, Tenney packed the infected hoof, then covered it with a leather patch made from a woman's shoe sole.

"I set a pattern that I hoped would get him up to the Derby," Tenney said. "I spaced his works five days apart. That's why I scratched him in the Derby Prep

(February 11). I'd have loved to run him, knowing he should have a race, but it came right between his work program. I decided it was best to train him for the race."

Adding a further element of uncertainty to the Santa Anita Derby was the absence in the saddle of Shoemaker, who was committed to Blue Ruler, ranked fourth on the Experimental at 123 pounds.

"I wanted to ride Blue Ruler in the Del Mar Futurity," Shoemaker said, "which we won, and I told the trainer that if he let me ride him at Del Mar, I would ride him back in the Santa Anita Derby."

John Longden, whose pumping style did not suit Swaps, was tabbed to pilot the colt.

The week of the Santa Anita Derby, which would offer a winner's purse of more than $90,000 from its $137,500 gross, Ellsworth received and considered two offers to sell Swaps. One offer was for $250,000, from out of state, and the other was for $200,000 from a Californian.

Ellsworth turned down the $250,000. But he wanted to counter the man who had made the lower offer by agreeing to accept it if he also could get a share of the pot won by Swaps in the Santa Anita Derby.

But no deal was struck after buyer and seller failed

to make telephone contact. After the race, Ellsworth finally encountered the interested buyer, who told him he would have accepted the deal. But by then it was too late. (The man who made the higher offer, Texan Lawrence Pollack, later bought Ellsworth's homebred Terrang, who at age six won his tenth stakes at Santa Anita, a record for the Arcadia track.)

While Ellsworth was wheeling and dealing on the Friday before the Santa Anita Derby, Tenney was trying to be as calm as possible back at the barn in Arcadia. "I put a new set of plates on Swaps Friday morning," he said. "He has a very thin shell on his right fore foot and believe me, my heart was in my mouth when I set the nails."

So the stage was set. Ellsworth and Tenney would send over a colt short of work, needing a race, ridden by a jockey who had never been on his back, running a mile and one-eighth in his first race around two turns, over a drying out track still dull from mid-week rain.

In the walking ring Tenney said to Longden, "I'm not gonna tell you how to ride a horse, Johnny, but I will tell you two things: lay behind the early pace as long as you want to and when the time comes he wants to run, let him run and keep him running."

Swaps won, but it was no picnic. Longden, who had turned forty-five earlier in the week, said, "Swaps was pretty rank early — full of run and I couldn't hold him." Lack of recent activity had left Swaps too fresh.

Longden had Swaps third early, as first stablemate Bequeath and then Right Down set the pace. Swaps made his move around the far turn and came into the lane three lengths on top. Longden said Swaps eyed the starting gate in the stretch, tried to prop (plant his feet), and then bore out, costing him considerable momentum.

The Pumper re-established control inside the furlong grounds and kept Swaps going as he drifted back toward the inside. Swaps was able to prevail by a half-length over Jean's Joe, a stablemate of Blue Ruler, who finished three and a half lengths farther back in third. The time of 1:50 was slow, but it did not take a professional to realize the rain-soaked strip was still drying out.

Post race, neither the media nor track publicists were able to get much of a rise out of either Ellsworth or Tenney. Courteous and thankful, both stone-faced horsemen were noncommittal about plans for the Kentucky Derby.

Ellsworth said, "We haven't talked about it. It depends on a lot of things and particularly how Tenney feels about it."

Tenney wanted to think about it and said, "But I'll listen to Mr. Ellsworth. There's no better judge of horses any place, and I don't bar the world."

The cowpokes from the Gila River Valley had just won their first hundred-grander, but they were not drunk with glory.

After a big win, they were likely to return to the ranch, have dinner at home, and maybe work leather at their own individual benches in the big leather room. Or they might trim a few more horses' feet outside. No matter if it was dark. Tenney always told Nola he could tell that Ellsworth was happiest when he was working outside at night, because he would start humming a cowboy tune.

Cold, sober, and always professional, Ellsworth and Tenney would watch a race without emotion. When it was over, if they had won, one or the other might smile.

The strict Mormon upbringing of Ellsworth and Tenney by parents who worked hard jobs in the dusty desert during the Great Depression offered little room for an extravagance of emotions.

Was Swaps legit? Was he Kentucky Derby material? Was it the track that accounted for the slow time? Would the race advance him or set him back? Did he have the requisite experience for the Derby? Would Shoemaker have ridden him better? Would the foot hold? How would he get to Louisville?

In 1955 there were seventy-seven days between the Santa Anita and the Kentucky Derby. First, Ellsworth and Tenney had to figure out whether Swaps was good enough to win the Run for the Roses and whether his foot would prevent him from being dead fit on the first Saturday in May.

Swaps' connections did not want to embarrass themselves or California by coming to the Kentucky Derby with a horse lacking in class or fitness. The difference between success and failure in racing in most cases rests on an ability to be realistic in the placement of one's horses. The Kentucky Derby is notorious as a showcase for horses that do not belong.

Ellsworth and Tenney concluded that Swaps probably was good enough, based on the Khaled colt's having won the Santa Anita Derby while short of training and experience. With more than two and a half

months between races, Tenney thought he had plenty of time to deal with the colt's foot ailment.

The owner and trainer decided to keep Swaps in California, train him up to the May 7 classic and ship him by train to Kentucky.

Tenney prepared two trials. To determine whether the colt was truly fit, he planned a mile workout twenty-four days before the Kentucky Derby. To prime the colt for the race, he planned to run him seven days before the Derby at Churchill Downs.

On April 13 at Hollywood Park, Swaps worked a mile under regular exercise rider Charlie White. Reeling off fractions of :46 3/5 and 1:10 2/5, Swaps completed the distance in 1:36, with a final furlong in :12 3/5.

"The clocker Pat Garrity told me it was the best mile work he had ever seen," said Bob Benoit, a young publicist at Hollywood Park at the time.

Tenney told Ellsworth after the sensational time trial that Swaps was ready. The trainer gave his colt one more stamina-building move — one and one-eighth miles in 1:51 — then joined him on a boxcar headed for Kentucky.

CHAPTER 5

Invader From The West

William Shoemaker steered Swaps through the colt's career with a finesse matched only by Swaps' fluent stride, but the partnership got off to a clumsy start. A late arrival to the scene, Shoemaker had not ridden Swaps until the colt's sixth and final start at two.

When Swaps knocked the rider into the rumble seat with a sudden move on the turn in the San Vicente, his first start as a three-year-old, budding superstar Shoemaker realized before hitting the wire that he had made a terrible mistake earlier by committing to ride Blue Ruler in the Santa Anita Derby.

Harry Silbert, the only agent Shoemaker ever had, was able to get the rider back aboard Swaps for the Kentucky Derby.

Swaps was scheduled to prep over the Churchill

Downs strip seven days before the Kentucky Derby in the six-furlong Jefferson Purse.

Two days beforehand, riding a $3,200 claimer for trainer Reggie Cornell in the first race at Golden Gate Fields, Shoemaker was thrown. By the time he arrived in Louisville, his right knee was so swollen and painful he could not bend it.

Veterinarian Dr. Alex Harthill took Shoemaker to the University of Louisville's athletic trainer, who drained fluid from the knee and administered physical therapy to the joint.

"I couldn't bend the knee," Shoemaker said. "I had to lower the stirrup to ride Swaps that day."

Swaps was training at Churchill Downs with purpose. A week before the Jefferson he covered five-eighths through deep mud in 1:01 2/5, moving trainer and veteran "Derby watcher" Jake Lowenstein to call it the best pre-Derby drill under the conditions he had ever seen.

For Shoemaker's lone mount of the day, Tenney instructed the ailing rider to make Swaps go as slowly as possible early and as fast as possible late. Five horses lined up for the five-thousand-dollar Saturday afternoon allowance race.

Conceding from eight to thirteen pounds and carrying 123 pounds, Swaps went off at 3-10 odds and was favored for the first time while making the ninth start of his career. Although Shoemaker restrained the red colt, Swaps was soon in front, setting the pace in :23 and :46 2/5. When The Shoe turned him loose under "mild urging," Swaps led the spread-eagled field, winning by eight and a half lengths.

Final time was 1:10 1/5, a tick off Bernwood's 1951 track record and a full second faster than five-year-old Torch of War needed to get the distance a race later carrying ten pounds less in the Churchill Downs Handicap.

"I told Shoemaker to ride Swaps out the full mile," Tenney said. "Actually, he only did it for seven-eighths and then stood up in his stirrups. However, it worked out all right. Swaps galloped out the mile and an eighth on his own."

Swaps was unofficially timed going out seven-eighths in 1:22 3/5, which equaled the track record, and out a mile in 1:36 1/5.

"Ellsworth was hopeful when he sent Swaps back to Kentucky," said Dr. Jock Jocoy. "But when Swaps ran fast over the Churchill Downs track, Rex called up the

ranch and said 'I think we're going to win the Kentucky Derby.' "

As was invariably the case with Swaps, things changed from day to day. The Thursday before the Kentucky Derby, Swaps could not put weight on his tricky foot, forcing Tenney to scrub what was supposed to be his final workout.

Tenney contemplated scratching Swaps from the Derby. Later in the day he had a brainstorm — although he had shod the colt no less than six times since arriving in Louisville, Tenney decided to file the hoof at a new angle and replace the makeshift leather sole, in hopes of relieving pressure from the inflamed spot.

"Tenney was about as good a blacksmith as there ever was," said Arnold Pessin, a Kentucky racetrack veterinarian at the time.

Swaps was sent out for a short breeze the morning before the Kentucky Derby. The foot passed the test with flying colors.

"I must've got it right this time," Tenney said.

On the Thursday before the Kentucky Derby, tragedy struck Shoemaker hard. Richard Hyatt (Red) McDaniel, a Bay Area trainer instrumental in igniting the rider's career, leaped to his death from the San Francisco Bay Bridge twenty minutes after saddling a winner at Golden Gate Fields.

Training winners came naturally to McDaniel, who led the national trainers' standings the previous five consecutive seasons. But the forty-four-year-old had been in ill health. It was an emotional blow to the shy man the press had dubbed Silent Shoe. McDaniel had been a mentor. Shoemaker later heard that McDaniel had left word to wish him luck in the Kentucky Derby.

Shoemaker continued physical therapy at the University of Louisville.

"The pain and swelling subsided, and my leg was more flexible when Derby Day arrived," he said. "At least I could bend it to a normal riding position."

Shoemaker wanted more than anything to be as right as he could for the Kentucky Derby, because Tenney and Ellsworth had come to realize Swaps was an immensely more potent charge for the Run for the Roses than he had been a couple of months earlier for the Santa Anita Derby.

The Khaled colt had sprung to life in the San Vicente. His nascent foot ailment, however, had retard-

ed his preparation for the Santa Anita Derby, in which he was short of training and experience around two turns. He had won that day on raw talent and class.

Swaps was no longer a gangly stripling. Stripped for action, he exuded power, especially around his deep girth, which showed considerable condition, without the hint of a rib. This was a heavyweight bout, and when Tenney took off Swaps' robe, he revealed a colt in breathtaking shape. The "left coast" challengers knew full well the responsibility they had in carrying the dreams and wishes of California owners, breeders, and fans.

Failed post-WWII invasions by well-fancied, highly publicized California-breds such as Your Host embarrassed Western racing professionals and dashed the hopes of Golden State racing fans of ever being able to beat Eastern bluebloods in the Run for the Roses again. (Although not a California-bred, Determine, the 1954 Kentucky Derby winner, was based in California.)

Hoping to end a thirty-three-year drought, Harry Geisen of Munster, Illinois, sent Tenney a rose from the garland that had been placed around the neck of Morvich in the winner's circle in 1922.

It was not with mock seriousness that Tenney had

promised Geisen that he would let Swaps smell the faded rose before he sent Swaps over to the paddock.

Tenney was not normally a sentimental man. He did not rely on a good-luck talisman. He made his own luck. Rarely had there been a horse more schooled for his task at Churchill Downs than Swaps.

In the days before the Derby, Tenney saw to it that Swaps covered as much of the Churchill Downs grounds as possible to familiarize the colt with the sights and sounds of the layout.

Tenney kept a radio with the volume turned up high near the colt's stall to prepare him for the blaring call to the post and attendant singing of "My Old Kentucky Home."

One fear Tenney had about Swaps on the day of the Kentucky Derby was the positioning of the starting gate after the field had been dispatched.

"What I'm afraid of," Tenney said, "is that my horse will come around that final turn, see the starting gate tucked away in the corner, and mosey over to see what it is. What I'm gonna do is ask Tom Young, the track superintendent, to bring out the gate on the morning of Derby day. Then I'm gonna walk Swaps past it a couple of times so that he'll be used to seeing it there. He's so observant that he'd notice a spot on your coat."

The Westerners' confidence in their representative was tempered mightily by the knowledge that William Woodward Jr.'s Belair Stud colorbearer Nashua provided the stiffest possible barrier to their colt's becoming the first California-bred to win the Derby since Morvich.

When asked by Turf writers in the days leading to the Kentucky Derby how good a colt he thought Nashua was, Eddie Arcaro answered with a question — "How can anybody tell?"

Nashua was so good in winning all four of his preps, including the Flamingo Stakes and Florida Derby, Arcaro himself could not gauge just how good he was.

The crop's champion colt at two, Nashua had his last Kentucky Derby prep in New York's Wood Memorial, in which he beat his long-time Eastern rival Summer Tan, who would enter the starting gate as the third choice for the Run for the Roses.

Nashua had lost only twice in eight starts at two. A big brute of a colt, Nashua gave the impression he had unlimited potential.

Summer Tan was a top colt in his own right. He had beaten Nashua in track-record time at two in the Cowdin Stakes at Aqueduct, but a serious illness in November had set him back considerably.

Professional horsemen familiar with both Nashua and Summer Tan considered Nashua primed for a top effort in the Kentucky Derby. On the other hand, they thought Summer Tan had not flourished over the winter and, although he had started to come around before the Wood, the strain of facing Nashua in that race actually set him back.

The first Saturday in May in 1955 began promisingly enough with sunny skies. As often happens as the day rolls on in the Ohio Valley, dark thunder clouds gathered, humidity increased noticeably, and the temperature rose. The thermometer hit eighty-five degrees.

The skies were foreboding enough for Tenney to call an audible on the line of scrimmage a few minutes before Swaps was scheduled to leave for the paddock.

Former track runner Tenney put some spikes on his colt's shoes to help him better grip the racing surface in case of an off track.

A cannoning of thunder set the Derby runners to

dancing after they were saddled. When the three-year-olds stepped onto the track and the band struck up "My Old Kentucky Home," all of the horses became highly animated, including Swaps. The Ellsworth colt settled down at once, though, indicating at least some of his schooling was paying dividends.

Size of the Derby field was small at ten runners, reflecting the prowess of Nashua. Swaps surprisingly opened as the favorite after the first day's betting, but by post time Nashua was the $1.30 to the dollar choice over Swaps at $2.80.

As the field paraded past the stands, bolts of lightning from the edge of a storm lit up the dark sky and unnerved the runners. The darkened skies and violent weather made the afternoon reminiscent of the climactic scene in John Taintor Foote's classic Kentucky racing story, "The Look of Eagles."

Reacting to one particularly vivid lightning strike, Nashua spun around, almost dropping Eddie Arcaro, who had to be assisted by a rider on a pony. A light drizzle, which began when the runners were being saddled, turned to a mist that did not appreciably alter the racing surface as the field entered the starting gate.

Before giving Shoemaker a leg up in the paddock, Tenney had told him to use his own judgment, but pointedly suggested it would be best to take Swaps off the pace.

When the gates opened, Nashua broke on top. Eddie Arcaro immediately held Nashua back, and Swaps, with Shoemaker tugging the reins, inherited the lead.

"I didn't try to steal this race," Shoemaker said. "I would have been content to get close up. But when none of the big horses showed any desire to set the pace, I quickly picked it up."

Arcaro did not mind that Shoemaker had taken the lead. Nashua's eighty-one-year-old trainer James "Sunny Jim" Fitzsimmons ("I don't ship well anymore") had told him on the telephone from New York to "cater to Summer Tan," Nashua's rival from the East.

Swaps was full of run and, under light rating from Shoemaker, was allowed to get away with a tepid first quarter in :23 3/5. Swaps took his field around the turn in :47 2/5 and continued easily to reach three-quarters on top in a moderate 1:12 2/5.

Only pressure applied to Swaps up to the half-mile pole came from 51-1 long shot Trim Destiny, the Arkansas Derby winner who offered a mild challenge a

couple of times. The stage was now set for the race the 100,000 fans had come to see.

Nashua, tracking in third, and Summer Tan, just behind him in fourth, were perfectly poised to make their bids.

At this point, Shoemaker thought, "Well, if they just let me go a little farther like this, they'll never catch me."

Shoemaker got his wish. Arcaro waited another furlong to jack up Nashua for his run. Content that he had Summer Tan under control, Arcaro asked Nashua for a run with three-eighths to go and the tall, powerful son of Nasrullah responded by moving up on the outside to mount his challenge. Nashua cut the margin to a half-length at the quarter pole. Summer Tan was just a length back in third.

Acutely aware that the crux of the race was upon them, writers fell silent in the press box. The only sound was that of *Daily Racing Form* trackman Don Fair calling out the positions as the runners hit the quarter pole at the top of the long homestretch.

Swaps raced relaxed to that point with his ears pricked. "But just at the quarter pole, those ears flattened," Shoemaker said, "and in a flash I caught the picture. He had seen the starting gate. It scared him and he was ready to prop — I felt sure of it.

"So I gave him the hardest belt I could muster, and he picked up his speed, pricked his ears again, and we were off in the nick of time."

Nashua got up to the middle of Swaps' body and remained lapped on his rival from the quarter pole until just past the furlong pole. "I knew they were coming," Shoemaker said. "I guess I could've reached out and touched his nose. I went to the whip and Swaps started to pull away. I knew the first inch he gained on Nashua that the race was ours."

Swaps, still fresh after a modest mile in 1:37, had plenty left and spurted clear inside the final furlong to win by one and a half lengths.

"Swaps led Nashua by a length and a half at the end, but that margin does not truly represent the amazing clarity of Swaps' score," Evan Shipman wrote in his *Daily Racing Form* column. "In our eyes, the invader from the West was not only 'handy' at the Derby finish, but was also fresh and in shape to have gone on from there."

Shoemaker attributed the victory to his mount's being able to take advantage of a moderate pace and Arcaro's concentrating on Summer Tan, who wound up more than six lengths behind Nashua in third.

Much was made of Fitzsimmons' warning to Arcaro about Summer Tan, but before the race Arcaro told *Sports Illustrated*'s Whitney Tower, "I don't think we'll have as much trouble from Summer Tan as from Swaps. He's the horse to beat."

Credit belonged in considerable measure to Shoemaker, who had given an early glimpse of what would become his two hallmarks, namely an ability to get the most out of a horse while bothering it the least and a knack of saving something for the stretch drive.

The authority with which Swaps won left no room for excuses. On the bare face of the result, the facts were impressive: the final half-mile in :49 2/5 was the fastest run in the eighty-one-year-old history of the classic, and the final time of 2:01 4/5 was only two-fifths of a second slower than Whirlaway's stakes standard.

Mesach Tenney rewarded himself that evening by switching his bunk for the first time in two weeks from the straw floor in the stall next to Swaps to the back-seat of his car. When he got up the next morning, he would awake to a world that would never be the same for either himself or his boyhood chum Rex Ellsworth.

CHAPTER 6

Iconoclasts

R acing in North America was conducted on a broad front in 1955, as tracks carding contests lay between the Pacific Coast and the Atlantic Seaboard and from the Great Lakes to the Gulf of Mexico.

Yet when it came to choosing sides between Swaps and Nashua, racing fans seemed to break along lines not entirely geographic. It was the wild and wooly West versus the East — and the East was anything right of Arizona.

Polarity between the camps siding with Swaps or Nashua was not based solely on the racing qualities of the two brilliant battlers, but on sectional pride or economic considerations.

The degree of animosity expressed by the two sides as to the superiority of Swaps versus Nashua, however, reached uncharted depths of intensity, in great part kindled by an increased competition among an expanding media.

Fueling the rhetoric was a realization by some of Nashua's supporters that Swaps' connections presented a genuine threat to the Eastern Establishment's stranglehold on the racing game, from the blood that ran through the veins of their prized stock to the traditional methods that had been cultivated over the years to develop top-class racehorses.

For the first time since the turn of the century, when E.J. "Lucky" Baldwin and James Ben Ali Haggin's runners succeeded with a frontal attack on the East's best steeds, Westerners sensed they finally had an outfit and a charger who would let them root on an equal footing with any representative of the East.

It was with agonizing distaste that Nashua's fans greeted the vision of their standard-bearer failing to land a knockout blow against Swaps in the Kentucky Derby. They wanted a rematch — and they wanted it under traditional circumstances: on their own turf in one of the remaining spring classics.

So when Ellsworth and Tenney announced they were passing up the last two-thirds of the Triple Crown and were heading home to California, the Establishment felt snubbed. The Eastern press took off the gloves and went at the Swaps team bare-fisted.

Quaint pieces in the press about Swaps' very own trainer doubling as a blacksmith and using the sole of a "lady's shoe" to cover the colt's ailing hoof gave way to shocking tales of how shabbily the Kentucky Derby winner was handled by his connections and how little regard Ellsworth and Tenney had for such a prized possession as a Thoroughbred.

One of the first stories to circulate was the one that had Tenney, mounted on a Western saddle, riding Swaps to the racing office and leaving him tied to a hitching post while he went for the mail.

Germination of the tale most likely sprang from the time when Swaps, ridden with a racing saddle by exercise rider Chester White and accompanied by Tenney mounted on a pony, was seen covering many miles on the Churchill Downs backstretch as he was schooled in the days prior to the Kentucky Derby.

Tenney and Ellsworth did not seek publicity. When approached by the media, they courteously and patiently explained their methods. They were humble. However, the Eastern press characterized them as rough-around-the-edges ranchers who treated their

stock like cattle, having little regard for the intelligence of the animal, and cocky enough to act as if they had reinvented the game.

As is generally the case in such matters, the truth checked in somewhere between.

Sure, they were cowboys — even to a point of wearing spurs on their boots inside their homes. Yes, some methods they used in their horse operation came from running cattle. And their techniques compared with timeworn practices in racing not only were out of the ordinary, some were downright shocking.

Many in the press made the mistake of branding them as uncaring or swell-headed. The cowboys did not minimize the mental capacities of horses. They simply espoused a philosophy in handling horses that was developed and considered normal on the Arizona cattle range.

"Rex Ellsworth never showed any elation or dejection after a race," said Tom Bell. "My dad once said to him 'You look like an Indian,' because he was so stone-faced."

Bell might have changed his mind if he had seen Ellsworth after Swaps won the Kentucky Derby, because the tall horseman was so rocked by the import of the event, he revealed afterward, that he was shaking uncontrollably. A well-read man, Ellsworth fully recognized the significance of his achievement and its place in the history of the game.

But the dignity and humility of the two horsemen were ignored in favor of stories that exaggerated some of their unorthodox horsemanship and placed them and their horse in a lesser light.

When Tenney showed up at Churchill Downs, he brought with him an entire ration of food that had been prepared for Swaps by Ellsworth in California.

Eyebrows were raised when Swaps was fed pellets instead of the traditional hay and oats. The pellets were characterized as unnatural, hard to digest, and somehow lacking in nutrition. In fact, the pellets contained an array of micronutrients that put Ellsworth decades ahead of his peers. He was the first major breeder in America to feed pellets.

Swaps was not hot-walked after exercise. Tenney's riders would stay mounted for about thirty-five minutes, allowing a horse to cool out while they remained in the saddle. The horse would then be walked directly into the stall, where hay would be waiting, spread out on the ground.

Tenney did not use hay racks or hay nets. "Everything is on the floor," he said. "I think it helps a horse to eat or do anything else with his head down. It improves his circulation."

Tenney, unlike other Kentucky Derby trainers, never took Swaps out to graze on the patch of grass that bordered Longfield Avenue, preferring to feed the California alfalfa he had brought with him. "Look at that alfalfa," he said. "That's sun-dried alfalfa grown on irrigated land. The best hay in the world."

Tenney fed Swaps twice a day (at 4 a.m. and 3 p.m.) at a time when conventional wisdom said three times was better. "I don't see no advantage to feeding more than twice a day," Tenney said. "Fact is, I suppose, you could feed only once."

When Swaps returned to the barn after training, no hot steaming buckets of water awaited for a bath, because there rarely was a bath. On days when a bath was deemed necessary, a garden hose was turned on the horse. Observers new to Tenney's methods thought the cowboy was either lazy or lacked the horsemanship to tend to a Thoroughbred properly.

"Back then no one in the East had ever seen anybody turn a hose on a racehorse," said Tommy Bell. "Today it is the norm."

When Swaps returned from the track in the morning, he was allowed to drink as much water as he wanted. "When a horse is not hot, you can let him drink all he wants," explained Tenney.

Unlike Eastern horsemen who wrapped the legs of their prized Thoroughbreds in standing bandages of clean white cotton, Tenney did not use wraps, leading critics to note that horses in the Ellsworth string were not pampered.

"We pamper our horses," Tenney countered, "if you mean that good food, good care, and the right kind of exercise is pampering."

Even the blacksmith's union got into the act, complaining that Tenney's shoeing of the Ellsworth horses took jobs away from its members.

Ellsworth was not spared scrutiny or ridicule either. In one interview, he was quoted out of context as saying that horses were dumb. He had to use a subsequent interview to set the record straight, explaining that he meant to say horses were not dumb (in fact, some were pretty smart), they just were not as intelligent as some other animals, such as pigs.

Relying on their understanding of the horse from their experience on the range, they tried to create a simple life for their animals. They did this by seeking to control the environment, sustenance, and behavior of their stock.

Tenney, in one example of implementing what he called the "Arizona Method," wanted horses to stay away from the door of their stalls. He thought horses preferred not to be annoyed by humans and should be allowed to relax alone as much as possible. To promote their solitude, Tenney used a piece of hose to bop the head of any horse appearing at the front of a stall.

"I remember one time when a filly was acting up in the shed row in Chicago," said Howard Battle, later the racing secretary at Keeneland. "Mish went out and hit it right between the eyes with an axe handle. It was different, but it worked for him."

He also recalled watching the races at Arlington Park one afternoon in a box next to Tenney when a spill left jockeys scattered on the turf and horses running loose.

"Mish sprinted down to the track, pushed a rider off a pony, got up, and quickly caught two of the loose horses," he said. "It was like something right out of a movie."

The media's scrutiny did not stop at the racetrack.

The new national magazine *Sports Illustrated* showed up right on the front doorstep of Ellsworth's home on the ranch. A feature story mentioned that not so much as a tree or a blade of grass grew on the entire three hundred acres of the Chino property.

"The old talk about horses having to be raised on that Kentucky bluegrass is just a lot of baloney," Ellsworth said when pressed. "I've raised good horses in California in paddocks where there's absolutely nothing on the ground for them to eat and everything they get is in their bin."

Clearly writing for readers outside of California (whose mass transportation did not include an underground rail network), Jim Murray in *Sports Illustrated* noted that Khaled ("the world's most valuable piece of horseflesh") "lived in a virtual sandpit about the size of a subway platform."

Murray wrote, "One end is walled in by his plaster-walled barn with holes in it. On the other end is a wire fence over which can frequently be seen hanging the ranch hands' wet wash. To Khaled it makes no difference, but the effect on the outsider is one of finding the Koh-i-noor diamond resting in a dirty shot glass."

California racing men and breeders, acting out of jealousy when unable to beat Ellsworth on the track or compete with his prized stallion in the breeding shed, added fuel to the fire by gossiping that he regularly registered foals born prior to January 1 and his mares were impregnated using artificial insemination.

As with most gossip, especially when it concerned the Ellsworth Ranch, facts did not support the contentions. Fast, well-grown two-year-olds owed their gate speed and size to a successful program of breaking and scientific feeding. There was talk that Ellsworth had been under investigation by The Jockey Club, yet the number of Khaled's foals, when analyzed on a percentage basis by the number of mares he bred, was not large in comparison to other stallions.

Stories about Ellsworth and Tenney would follow them around the racing and breeding world for the rest of their lives.

CHAPTER 7

"Halls of the mighty"

H ollywood Park is not in Hollywood. It is nineteen
miles south, in Inglewood. A lot of what com-
prises "Hollywood" is not physically located in that Los
Angeles neighborhood. The bulk of the mythical
aspects that contribute to the aura of Tinseltown is generated in nearby communities.

So when, in 1938, members of the motion-picture
industry opened a racetrack that provided recreational
escape from the doldrums of the city and the sour
memories of the Great Depression, naming it
Hollywood Park made sense.

Hollywood Park knew how to package entertainment
and spin a dream. Its original board of directors included
entertainment giants Al Jolson, Raoul Walsh, and Jack
Warner. With promoters like Mervyn LeRoy, James
Stewart, and Lanny Leighninger, and publicists like Al

Wesson and Bob Benoit, the suburban Los Angeles track was an ideal machine for bringing attention to the most exciting Thoroughbred to race in California since pari-mutuel wagering began at Santa Anita in 1933.

In 1955 and 1956, following Swaps' victory in the Kentucky Derby, the native son made ten starts in California, all but one of them at the plant dubbed the track of the "lakes and flowers."

"Al Wesson knew how to get ink," said Bob Benoit. "He was at USC during the football heyday of Howard Jones and the track and field dynasty of Dean Cromwell. He rode the trains back to South Bend for the Notre Dame games with all of the great writers and columnists of the day. He was pals with Grantland Rice, Jimmy Cannon, Red Smith — all of the great ones.

"When Swaps came along, he hired a guy named Joey Goldstein, a New York publicist who was skilled at planting columns back East. If Al had something to work with, he knew what to do with it."

The pairing of Wesson and Benoit seemed an odd one, as the boss had directed publicity at the University of Southern California. Protégé Benoit was a recent graduate of cross-town rival University of California at

Los Angeles, where as sports editor of UCLA's *Daily Bruin* he incorporated selections for local racetracks. It was Benoit's passion for racing that allowed him to cross enemy lines and land a job at Hollywood Park.

Publicity and promotion built the movie industry and, to a certain extent, Hollywood Park. When Swaps returned from Louisville, Wesson and Benoit were ready for him. They made sure there was a big welcome, plenty of press to cover it, and an attractive photo opportunity with Hollywood Park's signature.

Swaps arrived via a Santa Fe railroad car that offloaded near 104th Street and Crenshaw Boulevard, a one and a half-mile van ride to the stable area. Hollywood Park's Dutch-clad "Goose Girl" mascot took time off from navigating the infield lakes in a specially designed Goose-styled craft to pose for photographers and greet the Ellsworths and the Tenneys at the railroad siding.

With Swaps safely ensconced in Tenney's barn on the Inglewood backstretch, it took Wesson no time at all to size up the nation's mood and formulate his game plan: it was East versus West. Hollywood Park's gladiator was Swaps.

Nashua was set to make his next start in the Preakness, which in 1955 was run three weeks after

the Kentucky Derby. CBS covered the Preakness.

Hollywood Park's management quickly prodded NBC to produce a live nationwide telecast of the Will Rogers Stakes, set for two days after the Preakness on a special Memorial Day card, in which Tenney planned to run Swaps.

"Eastern writers, strangely quiet for three weeks, began to live and breathe again," Leon Rasmussen wrote in *The Thoroughbred Record* following Nashua's victory in the Preakness. "Vocally and in print they began to take the 'Horse of the Year' stand for William Woodward's wonderful colt and make queer noises that sounded like 'we'll get that Californian next time.' "

Two days later, Swaps gave Wesson and the West's press corps some ammunition to quiet the Easterners.

The Eastern Establishment felt its traditions had been snubbed when Swaps skipped the Preakness. Ellsworth could have supplemented Swaps to the second leg of the Triple Crown, but no such provision existed for the Belmont. Ellsworth said he would have considered running in the Preakness if the Belmont had been viable. However, since there could be no Triple Crown, Ellsworth said he decided to take the colt back to California.

"Swaps' right hind ankle blew up after the Derby,"
Dr. Alex Harthill said. "Mish Tenney asked me to come
by and take a look at it. I injected it. A lot of water
squirted out of there. There was a lot of pressure. That's
the real reason they took him back home."

The red colt breezed a half-mile and three-quarters
of a mile at Hollywood Park after he returned from the
Kentucky Derby.

On a holiday that attracted 62,752 to the Inglewood
track, Swaps tracked stablemate Bequeath around the
clubhouse turn, got the lead curving for home, and
won the Will Rogers by twelve lengths.

The tangible facts of the race were that Swaps carried 126 pounds (conceding between four and twelve
pounds to five rivals) and his $2.30 payoff for a two-
dollar bet was the lowest at Hollywood Park since
Kentucky Derby hero Lawrin returned $2.20 at the
inaugural meeting seventeen years earlier. The final
time of 1:35 for the mile was a fifth of a second off the
track record that had been broken two days earlier and
equaled the previous track record. The impression of
the race was that, with Bill Shoemaker having a stout
hold on Swaps throughout the race, Swaps looked to

be every bit as impressive as Nashua had been two days earlier while taking the Preakness in record time.

When it had been revealed that Swaps would skip the Preakness, John Chandler wrote in the *Lexington Herald* that Swaps' "next race will be against cream-puffs in California." True enough, the Khaled colt did face lightweights in the Will Rogers. His next race was a different matter. His next race set him apart.

Mish Tenney told the press after the Will Rogers that he would bring Swaps back in two weeks against older horses in the Californian Stakes. Tenney said running against older horses was not ideal.

"However, Swaps is acting more seasoned with every race," Tenney said. "He used to have some distracting little habits, but now he's all business.

"I particularly like the way he took dead aim on the starting gate Monday when he was about one hundred yards away. He walked straight to it and was ready for the gun the minute the doors were slammed."

Swaps employed a stride in winning the Will Rogers that would be his hallmark. His action was pure and rhythmical. He seemed to barely touch the ground.

It was one thing to win with flawless action over a

hapless group of substandard three-year-olds. It was another thing to maintain a machine-like fluidity under the pressure of facing some of the top seasoned handicap performers in training.

Under the weight-for-age conditions of the Californian, Swaps carried the maximum of 115 pounds, receiving no weight concessions under the allowances for the race. Determine, who had won the Charles H. Strub Stakes equivalent in the Santa Anita Maturity, and the Kentucky Derby a year earlier, carried 126 pounds, the equivalent of the weight assigned to Swaps, considering their difference in age under the scale.

Those receiving weight concessions were Rejected, winner that year of the Hollywood Gold Cup and a year earlier of the Santa Anita Handicap; Mister Gus, who would win the next year's Woodward; Novarullah, an English stakes winner who placed in three important handicaps that season; and Travertine, winner that season of the Peninsula Handicap. Rejected received six pounds; the remainder, nine pounds.

Adding to the challenge was the absence in the saddle of Shoemaker, who was serving a riding suspension. Tenney reached out to Chicago for The Shoe's

replacement in journeyman rider Dave Erb.

Bettors in the crowd of 51,210 backed Swaps down to sixty-five cents on the dollar for the one and one-sixteenth-mile Californian, which carried a gross purse of $109,800. Determine, Mister Gus, and Rejected all were held at about 5-1 odds.

Mister Gus, fresh from setting a blistering :44 3/5 initial half when beaten less than a length in track-record time for a mile over the Hollywood Park strip, set the Californian pace, as Swaps tracked him while under a pull. Early fractions were :23 1/5 and :46. Determine followed in third.

Erb signaled to Swaps at the head of the lane by pushing on him with his hands that it was time to go after Mister Gus. The substitute rider did not use or show the whip to Swaps, whose superb action was not disturbed as he cruised past the sixteenth pole in 1:34.

From there to the wire, where Swaps arrived one and one-quarter lengths in front of Determine, Erb had taken him in hand. Afterward, Erb called the winner a "perfect machine."

The final time of 1:40 2/5 shaved two-fifths of a second from Poona II's world mark. Tenney told reporters that he was not surprised by the new standard, only at the ease with which it was accomplished.

"If there was any remaining doubt as to the eligibility of Swaps for a place among the best horses of the century, it was erased in the $100,000-added Californian Stakes," Joe Estes wrote in *American Racehorses of 1955*.

"The parallel of this performance — a 3-year-old in June beating a top-class field of older horses without a weight advantage — was beyond memory in American racing."

On an afternoon that earlier had seen Nashua crank up the debate over superiority by winning the Belmont Stakes by nine lengths, the regional rhetoric also was turned up a notch by Western writers.

"Swaps, the country's champion 3-year-old...," Paul Lowry wrote in the *Los Angeles Times*.

"Swaps achieved turf immortality today," United Press International's writer typed from the Hollywood Park press box.

"This was the race where Swaps entered the halls of the mighty," wrote Leon Rasmussen.

A month later Swaps made his final California start at three in the Westerner. Most of the interest in the

one and one-quarter-mile event occurred before the running, when Hollywood Park wrestled with whether to cancel wagering.

Hollywood Park officials feared a minus pool, in which the track would have to make up any shortfall resulting from the difference between the amount of money bet and the amount of the payoff in the event Swaps won the race.

Stewards officiating the meeting approved "win only" betting. To accommodate bettors, Hollywood Park added a new window at the bottom of the tote board where the morning line is listed to be able to show Swaps' odds of 1-10. In fact, final odds dropped to 1-20 for a payoff of $2.10 for a two-dollar wager.

Swaps justified the odds.

Reunited with Shoemaker, Swaps entered the gate with four rivals. He went to the front soon after the start, set the pace in hand, was allowed to show some speed once in the lane, and then was taken in hand through the final furlong.

Shoemaker said he never tried harder to pull a horse up than he did in the final furlong of the Westerner. Clocker Pat Garrity said he caught Swaps reaching the furlong pole in 1:47, which was a fifth of a second off the world record. Swaps finished out the trip in 2:00 3/5. He was ten lengths in front turning for home and won by six under 126 pounds.

After Swaps had won his eighth race in a row, Shoemaker pointed out that the Khaled colt had not been touched with a whip since winning the Kentucky Derby.

Rex Ellsworth told the press corps after the Westerner that Swaps would go to Chicago for the summer, to be followed by a campaign in the East. First on the agenda was the American Derby, run on grass at Arlington Park.

There had been a lot of talk and ink about a possible rubber match with Nashua, who also was headed to Chicago after taking the Dwyer at Aqueduct for his seventh victory in eight starts at three.

Ellsworth said he was neither looking for nor ducking Nashua. He said he would run where the purses were the biggest. If Nashua showed up, so be it. He thought Swaps was the pro tem national leader and it was up to Nashua to find Swaps and beat him if he wanted to reclaim the top spot in the rankings.

Immediately after Nashua had won the Belmont

and Swaps had taken the Californian, Ellsworth and Woodward appeared to have agreed on a series of match races, the first of which was to have taken place at Hollywood Park.

A misunderstanding in communications, however, quickly doused the plans, but not before both parties got their noses out of joint much to the delight of the press. Mervyn LeRoy interceded on behalf of Hollywood Park and met with both sides. Although he failed to get them to agree to a match race, he did get them to agree to a truce.

Al Wesson worked behind the scenes with LeRoy. The California racing industry had a potential champion in Swaps, and Wesson knew it better than anybody else. He realized that Hollywood Park's meeting was rapidly coming to an end and that if a match race did take place, it might come at a different venue.

Wesson and Benoit knew that any benefits from a meeting between Swaps and Nashua would accrue to Hollywood Park, so they worked tirelessly to keep their contacts in the media in touch with every twist and turn in any negotiations that might lead to a contest between the two colts.

CHAPTER 8

Three Good Feet

G iven the closeness of Hollywood Park and its show-business connections to the Swaps' camp, it is ironic that an actor whose signature role was that of Alexander Graham Bell made the telephone call that led to Washington Park's getting the match race between Swaps and Nashua.

One July evening in the summer of 1955, horse racing fan and owner Don Ameche chanced upon William Woodward Jr. at the 21 Club in Manhattan. When the star of stage and screen became aware that Nashua's owner seriously wanted to match his colt against Swaps, Ameche contacted his friend Benjamin F. Lindheimer, the owner of Washington Park racetrack in Chicago.

Lindheimer called Mish Tenney. The trainer spoke with Rex Ellsworth. After considerable negotiation an agreement was hammered out late one evening in a long-distance conversation that finalized what would be billed as the latest version of the "Match Race of the Century."

On July 20, 1955, details of the match race were revealed. The race would take place on the last day of August, with Washington Park putting up a purse of $100,000 at the Kentucky Derby distance of a mile and one-quarter under winner-take-all conditions.

Lindheimer had an edge over Hollywood Park, because previous negotiations broke down when Woodward became loathe to ship Nashua to California. Both sides considered Washington Park neutral territory.

Washington Park owned the longest homestretch in American racing at 1,531 feet. Legendary sports writer Red Smith described the oval as being configured like a paper clip, as the Chicago track had short, sharp bends and long straightaways.

Lindheimer also was lucky in that Nashua had just been to Chicago and Swaps was headed that way.

Nashua had won the Arlington Classic at Arlington Park the weekend before the announcement. "Sunny Jim" Fitzsimmons changed Nashua's schedule. He would skip the Travers Stakes, train Nashua at Saratoga, and not race the Nasrullah colt during the interim.

Swaps had won the Westerner at Hollywood Park the weekend before Nashua had taken the Classic. Tenney would alter Swaps' program to skip the Sunset Handicap, depart by rail a week after the announcement, and prep for the match race eleven days beforehand in the American Derby, carded on turf at one and three-sixteenths miles at Washington Park.

With forty-one days and a trip between races for Swaps, Tenney said he "let up" on the colt after they arrived in Chicago.

"He filled up on us a little more than we expected," Tenney said of a Swaps that had gotten a bit too heavy with a lack of activity.

Tenney felt pinched for time in preparing Swaps for his next two races. "I had to get this horse fit enough to win the American Derby in a shorter time than I normally would have used, and the problem was to have him fit enough to beat a field like he faced in the American, but not fit to the point where

it would have dulled him for the match race," he said.

Prior to the American Derby Tenney sent Swaps out for a pair of works on the grass, a surface over which the California colt had neither raced nor breezed. In his first work, he zipped five-eighths in :59 2/5. Undaunted by the fact that turf sprint races were few at the time, publicists nonetheless pointed out the clocking was a mere one-fifth of a second slower than the American record.

Swaps then breezed seven-eighths on grass in 1:23 4/5. The Washington Park publicity office reveled in being able to release the news that Swaps had broken the American record by a fifth of a second in a workout.

Five days later, Swaps, under top weight of 126 pounds, was twenty cents on the dollar to concede seven pounds to Traffic Judge and Honeys Alibi and thirteen pounds to three others for the $146,425 American Derby.

Swaps set the pace in hand, repulsing some mild challenges from 6-1 Parador. Shoemaker loosened his hold on Swaps, and the colt opened up by three lengths at mid-stretch, whereupon Shoemaker took

Swaps in hand again.

At the sixteenth pole Shoemaker stood in the saddle and turned around. When he noticed Traffic Judge closing on him, The Shoe lightly flicked Swaps with the whip. The Ellsworth colt picked it up a bit and won, in hand, by a length.

The final time of 1:54 3/5 set a new course record and equaled the American record set earlier in the season in the Arlington Handicap.

Shoemaker told Tenney that Swaps got tired. Tenney noted the next morning that Swaps was a lot "steadier" after the race than he had been going into it. Ellsworth thought Tenney had run a short horse in the American Derby.

If Tenney had pushed the accelerator on Swaps before the American Derby, then he floored it in the eleven days between the grass start and the match race. Six days after Swaps had run in American-record time on turf, Tenney sent the colt a mile on the main track at Washington Park with regular exercise rider Chester White in the tack in a startling 1:35.

A hard rain pelted the racing surface the morning before the match race. Tenney sent Swaps to the

Swaps, a striking burnished chestnut,
used his blazing speed to rewrite the
record books and become a hero to
California and the nation.

A son of the famed stallion Hyperion (above), Khaled (left) was purchased by Rex Ellsworth from the Aly Khan to stand at Ellsworth's California ranch. Swaps' dam, Iron Reward (below left), showed little on the racetrack but distinguished herself as a broodmare. Her sire, Beau Pere (bottom), was a top stallion for his owner, movie mogul Louis B. Mayer.

Boyhood friends Rex Ellsworth (on left) and Mesach Tenney combined their talents as horsemen to find success on the Turf. Their unconventional way of raising horses, termed the "Arizona Method" for their home state, included feed designed by Ellsworth and produced in a special mill on his California ranch. Swaps is shown feeding outside the mill (below).

Both Ellsworth and Tenney were expert farriers and did all of Swaps' shoeing (right). As a two-year-old, Swaps (above, with first jockey John Burton) was unspectacular, but he gave notice of greater things to come with a romp in his three-year-old debut, the San Vicente Stakes (below). New regular rider Bill Shoemaker was aboard in the San Vicente.

While short of training due to his recurring foot ailment, Swaps won the Santa Anita Derby (below) but still was not considered definite for the Kentucky Derby by his connections. The win was the first worth $100,000 for Ellsworth and Tenney (above, in the winner's circle).

Trainer Tenney familiarized
Swaps with Churchill Downs by
leading him around the backstretch the week before the
Derby (above, Tenney on pony,
right, and Chester White on
Swaps). In the Kentucky Derby,
Swaps gained the lead from the
start and never relinquished it,
even when challenged by rival
Nashua (right, Nashua on outside). Afterward, a victorious
Swaps heads back to the barn
(below).

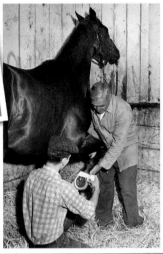

Skipping the Preakness and Belmont, Swaps returned to California, where he was met by Ellsworth (above). The colt's right front foot was still a concern (right, as grooms bandage the foot), but Swaps had no trouble winning the Will Rogers Stakes three weeks after the Derby (below).

With Shoemaker serving a riding suspension, Dave Erb was aboard Swaps in the Californian (below), in which the chestnut easily handled older horses, including 1954 Kentucky Derby winner Determine. Swaps followed with a gate-to-wire victory in the Westerner. The win was easy but Tenney couldn't help checking on Swaps' hoof (above).

Swaps next traveled to Chicago where he ran on the turf for the first
time, in the American Derby. He won by a length in what turned into
a prep for his famous match race with Nashua. But in the match race,
Swaps' problem foot acted up again. Nashua got an easy lead,
and the big chestnut never had a chance (below).

The match race was Swaps' final start at three. He returned to California to undergo surgery on his hoof. Tenney performed the procedure, cutting away the damaged area. Swaps was given time to recuperate (left, with exercise rider Chester White). Two weeks later, Tenney and Ellsworth discussed the status of Swaps' hoof (below, Tenney on left).

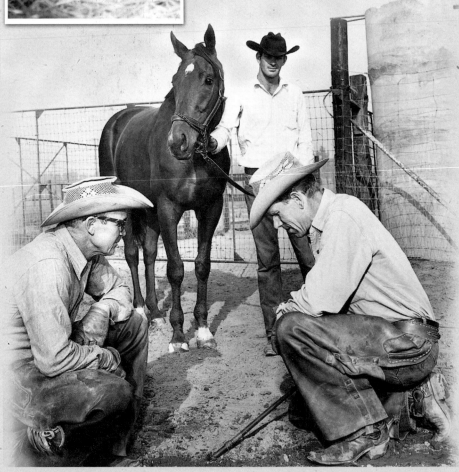

Swaps returned to racing in February of his four-year-old year,
winning an overnight handicap with his usual ease (above).
After missing the Santa Anita Handicap because of a wet track,
Swaps was sent to Florida where he gave the audience a world-
record performance in the Broward Handicap (below).

Returned to the familiar Hollywood Park grounds,
Swaps reeled off record-setting victories in the Argonaut,
Inglewood, and American handicaps. In the American
(above), U.S. Army General Omar Bradley (on far left) pre-
sented the trophy to Ellsworth and Tenney. In the Hollywood
Gold Cup (below), Swaps sped to a two-length score.

Swaps completed his record-setting run at Hollywood Park in the
Sunset Handicap (top). Sent back
to Chicago, Swaps ran a dismal
seventh in the Arch Ward at
Washington Park, then rebounded
to take the Washington Park
Handicap in what turned out to be
his final start. A month later
Swaps injured himself in a workout and was retired. Known for his
gentle disposition, Swaps shared a
tender moment with groom Josie
Kascendi (right).

After the Washington Park Handicap, Ellsworth revealed that he had sold half-interest in Swaps to John and Dorothy Galbreath (below), the owners of Darby Dan Farm in Lexington, Kentucky. After standing one season in California, Swaps was purchased outright by the Galbreaths and sent to Darby Dan.

Swaps had a quick start at stud with his best offspring coming from his early crops. Among his top performers were the champion two-year-old filly Affectionately (top), Kentucky Derby and Belmont winner Chateaugay (left), and champion handicap mare Primonetta (below).

Swaps concluded his stud career at Spendthrift Farm
alongside old rival Nashua. The chestnut speedster died in
1972 at the age of twenty. He was buried at Spendthrift
but the grave was later moved to the Kentucky Derby
Museum grounds at Churchill Downs (below).
At Hollywood Park, Swaps is remembered in bronze
the way he should be — in full flight.

1952   1972

SWAPS
WINNER OF 1955 KENTUCKY DERBY
LIFETIME EARNINGS $ 848,900

track for a blowout. The "California Comet" had completed his preparation.

In a period of fifteen days, Swaps had worked
seven-eighths on grass in 1:23 4/5, run nine and a
half furlongs on grass in American record time,
worked a mile on dirt in 1:35, and had a blow out. On
day sixteen he ran in the match race.

The buildup to the race as crafted by Lindheimer
and his staff equaled the import of the race, as
Washington Park pulled out all the stops. National
television and radio networks branched out as never
before to reach the American public. Dave Garroway
telecasted his two-hour, top-rated morning program,
"Today," from the track.

Fifteen hundred people reportedly lined up at the
turnstiles at Washington Park at 8:30 a.m., an hour
before the gates officially opened. Clubhouse lunches
were served in three shifts. Horsemen cooperated by
entering forty-eight hours in advance instead of
twenty-four so that the track would have enough
time to produce a lavish four-color souvenir program.

Seasoned racegoers characterized the mood at
Washington Park as upbeat and excited but nowhere

on a par with the party atmosphere of the Kentucky Derby. The match race was more of a serious affair, attended by fans more interested in the outcome of the race than in experiencing an event.

The uniqueness of the match race was that it got the non-racing and the casual fan involved in a horse race other than the Kentucky Derby. It seemed everybody in America knew about the contest.

All of the major participants showed up for this one: Ellsworth, Tenney, the debonair Eastern sportsman Woodward, and even eighty-one-year-old Sunny Jim Fitzsimmons, who had stayed home from the Derby and never stopped blaming himself for telling Arcaro to "cater to Summer Tan." He felt that he would have recognized Swaps as the horse to beat if he had seen him in the flesh at Churchill Downs.

"Banana Nose" Arcaro, at the top of his game, was dressed in the scarlet cap and red polka dot silks of Belair Stud. Willie "The Shoe" Shoemaker — age twenty-four, but already the heir apparent to "The Master" — wore the red jacket and black triangle colors of Ellsworth.

Match races were not new to Lindheimer. "I've

always been interested in match races," he said at the time. "In 1945 we staged a fine meeting between Busher and Durazna, two great fillies, while in 1947 we originated the Armed-Assault match.

"Assault was not training properly, and we were not interested in having the race here, just as I would rather sacrifice our investment in this event rather than permit it to go on with either contestant in anything but perfect condition."

Rain from the previous day left the track wet in places. Swaps and Nashua were saddled on the infield turf course next to lawn statues with each owner's colors painted on the respective jockey.

Swaps had never been saddled on a turf course in front of the stands before, so Tenney practiced the routine with him a few times in the days before the race.

Uncharacteristically, Swaps swished his tail and acted nervous while being saddled, even though he had been schooled to saddle on the turf course. Bettors in the crowd of 35,262 made Swaps the 3-10 favorite, with Nashua held at 6-5.

When the bell rang and the gates opened, Arcaro

popped Nashua out on top, nailed him at once with the whip, and steered the mahogany warship to the driest part of the track. Swaps swerved coming out of the gate, tried to bear out in the early running, and was relegated to racing on a wet part of the track.

Shoemaker had anticipated Arcaro would go for the lead. When Swaps got away from the gate so awkwardly though, most of his options were gone.

"Arcaro rode like the champ he was," said Shoemaker, "and even if he hadn't, I'm not sure that Swaps could have beat Nashua anyway. The mistake was mine. I made no excuses because Eddie Arcaro, The Master, just gave me a lesson."

Shoemaker urged Swaps to make three separate runs at Nashua in the first seven-eighths of the race. Each time Swaps closed the gap, Nashua pulled away. Shoemaker gave up in the stretch and eased Swaps. The first three-quarters was run in a fast 1:10 2/5. Nashua cantered home six and a half lengths on top in a slow 2:04 1/5.

Members of the Swaps' camp made no excuses following the race and were characterized in the media as being good losers all around.

"Swaps wasn't fit," Shoemaker later wrote. "I'm not making excuses, but the day after the race it came out that Swaps could hardly get out of his stall the morning of the race. He had an infection in his right front foot, and when Mish Tenney put him through a work the day before the race, he put a leather pad around the bad foot to protect it. The track came up muddy, after a heavy rain, and some mud got up inside the leather pad and made the infection worse.

"Mish Tenney went to see Ben Lindheimer. He told him the story. Mr. Lindheimer listened and then told Misch that he couldn't call the race off, too much was involved. The papers were calling it the 'dream race' and the public was all excited. Lindheimer said, 'We can't disappoint these people.'

"Mr. Ellsworth went along with the deal. Tenney called Harry (Silbert) and told him not to tell me about Swaps' sore foot. They figured that if I knew, I would pull up the first time Swaps took a bad step.

"As it was, I did pull up Swaps in the stretch, but that was when I knew he was beat. I think Ellsworth and Tenney thought Swaps could handle the situation even with a bad foot. When I was warming up Swaps before the race, I felt that his action wasn't right, but I thought it was because the track was muddy in spots."

The next day Ellsworth announced that Swaps' chronic weakness in the wall of his right fore foot was once again causing him soundness problems. Ellsworth informed the press that Swaps would have to undergo an operation.

Many of Nashua's supporters in the press thought Swaps' people were trying to diminish the great victory of their standard-bearer and said so in print.

Joe Estes, an insider with close ties to Ellsworth, validated the story of the inflamed foot in *American Racehorses of 1955*. He wrote, "Possibly he stepped on a rock. At any rate, the spot in the right fore foot was inflamed again. Ellsworth and Tenney, who almost certainly would have scratched the colt if it had been an ordinary race, held their counsel and took the risk. Only a few horsemen learned the situation before the race."

Summing up the match race, Estes said the result proved nothing more than "Nashua with four good feet was much better than Swaps with three."

Nashua was voted the champion of his generation at three and Horse of the Year. Swaps was done for the year, having won all eight of his starts prior to the match race.

CHAPTER 9

Better Than Ever

S waps had almost been lost as a racehorse following the Washington Park match because of his
damaged foot, which *Daily Racing Form*'s Charles Hatton
called the most famous since Achilles'. Shortly after
arriving at Ellsworth's Chino ranch, Swaps was subject-
ed to surgery.

Tenney, Ellsworth, ranch veterinarian Jock Jocoy,
and highly respected racetrack veterinarian Bernard J.
Errington met the morning of September 12 to discuss
the operation to take place later in the day. Such was
the respect for Tenney's skills as a blacksmith, the team
chose to use the trainer's steady and experienced hands
to guide the knife that pared and probed the inside of
Swaps' foot to a perilous depth.

Fortunately, the affected area stopped just short of
reaching the sensitive live tissue of the foot, a circum-

stance that would have necessitated the retirement of Swaps. Those involved hoped by cutting away all of the damaged area that the foot would regenerate normal tissue and be healthy once again.

Swaps recuperated at the Chino ranch. The coronet band right above the bad foot was blistered to stimulate more rapid growth. His ankles were blistered to tighten his joints. The colt was sent to Tenney's barn at Santa Anita around Thanksgiving Day, with a plan that called for Swaps to point for the February renewal of the San Antonio Handicap as a steppingstone to the Santa Anita Handicap.

Tenney said he was given a ninety-day job to perform in seventy days. Ellsworth said the foot had grown out well, but until pressure was applied to it, nobody would know for sure if the hoof would be all right.

The trainer liked what he saw when Swaps arrived. "He's bigger and stronger than he was last year and is still developing," Tenney remarked.

Tenney had tried to fit a square peg into a round hole when rushing Swaps to make the match race with Nashua. He poured an inordinate amount of work into the elegant colt in a very short time. Such was his mania to insure the colt was perfectly primed for the important match that Tenney gambled on breezing the colt with the suspect foot on a wet track the morning before the race. It backfired when Swaps not only was unable to run his race in the match but was through for the year.

As a four-year-old Swaps would be handled more conservatively by Tenney.

Swaps also trained more impressively as a newly turned four-year-old. Tenney had to dance around wet tracks in the winter of 1956 at Santa Anita, but when he was able to find a safe track on which to work Swaps, the more powerful red colt really showed him something.

Swaps drilled seven-eighths in 1:24 in mid-January, a mere seven weeks and two days after returning to the barn. Tenney thought about using the early February seven-furlong San Carlos as a return engagement. He entered Swaps a day beforehand. Swaps, though, stayed in his stall because rain made the track suspect, and the morning of the race Tenney discovered that the old hoof injury had resurfaced.

"We are right back where we were a year ago at this time," he said, "only with the exception there is no infection now."

Tenney pared away some hoof that was not as firm as normal and once again put on a leather pad to protect it. The trainer was unable to get Swaps ready for the San Antonio. He was able to work him between races, though, and Swaps looked sharp under Chester White, cruising three-quarters in 1:10 2/5.

Trainer Charlie Whittingham, who saddled Mister Gus to take the San Antonio, was asked what he thought about the impending Big 'Cap after watching Swaps breeze. "If Swaps comes back good, we can't beat him," he said.

Eight days before the Santa Anita Handicap, Swaps came back good. He was brought over for an overnight race dubbed the L.A. County Fair Handicap. The field was formidable and included Bobby Brocato, Arrogate, Joe Jones, Traffic Judge, and Guerrero.

Rusty from his spate of inactivity, Swaps broke poorly but was soon traveling comfortably under Shoemaker, who kept a tight rein as the colt tracked early in fourth place. Shoemaker let Swaps run turning for home. When the colt easily opened a daylight advantage, The Shoe took him in hand to score by nearly two lengths.

Swaps won with his ears pricked in a style that once again sent Turf writers to their *Roget's Thesaurus* in search of superlatives. Their hero had returned seemingly every bit as good as when he impressed them as being the best three-year-old in America. Swaps' victory restored life to the dreams of his ardent admirers and lifted five months of depression.

Ellsworth and Tenney admitted they were amazed with how easily Swaps dispatched such a high-class field, because they knew they had run a short horse. The notion of the high quality of the field was validated the following weekend when Bobby Brocato — beaten pointedly while in receipt of three pounds from 127-pound top-weight Swaps in his comeback — romped in the Big 'Cap by six lengths.

Swaps was entered in the Santa Anita Handicap. Rain turned the strip wet, and Tenney entered Swaps more to keep his options open, rather than to be a probable starter. Tenney watched enough races on Big 'Cap day to judge that the slow, moist surface was not one over which he wanted to run his prized steed, so he scratched him two hours before post time. It was the third time that winter that Tenney showed restraint.

Following the Santa Anita meeting, Tenney took Ellsworth's best horses to Florida, where the owner and trainer hoped Swaps would run against Nashua in the Gulfstream Park Handicap.

Once again Swaps was not ready for the signature handicap event of the meeting. On a day when Nashua went down to defeat, Swaps breezed between races, zipping a half under Shoemaker in :46 2/5. Ellsworth said that Swaps would not run until Hollywood Park.

Ellsworth was playing a little hardball with Gulfstream officials, who readily responded to the Californian's needs not only by changing the dates of two races for Swaps and his three-year-old Kentucky Derby-bound stablemate, Terrang, but by raising the purses as well.

Both Ellsworth stars would appear back-to-back on the April 14 card, Swaps in the Broward Handicap and Terrang in the Miami Press Photographers Purse over the same distance of a mile and seventy yards.

It mattered little that Swaps was burdened for the first time with 130 pounds, because his connections were more interested in getting a race into him. The 20,345 attendees comprised the largest crowd ever to see a horse race at Gulfstream in the month of April. They were not disappointed as 3-10 favorite Swaps broke the world record by two-fifths of a second and the track standard by a full second with a clocking of 1:39 3/5.

Once again, those in attendance were taken aback, not so much by the record clocking as the manner in which it was accomplished. Shoemaker grabbed Swaps coming out of the gate and had his mouth pulled wide open as he restrained him while they rounded the first turn.

Two Fisted set the pace with a half in :45 3/5, tracked by Swaps. Under a constant tug by Shoemaker, who kept reaching for new holds at various stages of the race, Swaps was allowed to move to the pacesetter in the middle of the second turn.

Swaps collared the leader, took the final bend wide, and was under a stranglehold as his rider kept looking backward in the final sixteenth. Shoemaker eased him in the final thirty yards. He won by two and a quarter lengths, giving twenty-five pounds to runner-up Galdar.

The ease with which the California colt eclipsed the world record on Eastern soil gave writers on the "right coast" something to think about as the 1956 racing year moved pell-mell toward its busiest part of the season.

Tenney contemplated racing Swaps one more time in the East, but opted instead to bring the colt back home and prepare for the lucrative Hollywood Park meeting.

With six weeks to crank up the publicity machine, Hollywood Park was able to attract 58,801 for the May 26 renewal of the Californian, making it both the largest Saturday and most attended non-holiday crowd in the history of the Inglewood track.

Swaps had won the Californian a year earlier, carrying high weight on the scale. This time he carried one pound above the standard, sharing top weight of 127 pounds with Bobby Brocato. Bettors made Swaps the favorite at thirty-five cents on the dollar.

Such was the adoration of their hero that the fans on hand gave Swaps a series of ovations from the time he entered the paddock until he went into the starting gate. "We have never seen such a spontaneous exhibition of good will toward a horse since the days of Seabiscuit and Citation," Oscar Otis wrote in *Daily Racing Form*.

Admirers of Swaps came to participate in a coronation. What they witnessed was a beheading. The nose of Porterhouse struck the wire a head in front of Swaps. The beloved reinsman Shoemaker had done a disservice to the colt, the connections, and the collection of fans on hand by easing Swaps in deep stretch.

In a career that would end with more glory than for any other rider in the history of the Turf, The Shoe in the Californian made a blunder that would rank alongside his error in misjudging the finishing post at Churchill Downs aboard Gallant Man a year later when he stood up prematurely, probably costing his mount the victory in the Kentucky Derby.

Shoemaker's judgment call in the Californian, while causing his mount to lose, was not ill conceived. In riding Swaps, the jockey always knew his horse may have been short of work because of the chronically sore foot, and it was incumbent on him to make the colt's races as easy as possible in order to protect the weak hoof.

Shoemaker also had been able to fashion a commanding lead in deep stretch, which should have allowed him the luxury of not having to persevere with his mount all the way to the wire.

Bobby Brocato, the 3-1 second choice, set the pace of :23 and :45 3/5, followed closely by Swaps, who was always in hand. Swaps went to the pacesetter and moved by him before the quarter pole while continuing under a

tug. Bobby Brocato fought back gamely but fell back.

Shoemaker, three lengths on top aboard Swaps at the furlong pole, turned around, saw no apparent danger, and continued to ride only with his hands, as he eased Swaps a bit.

"Just as he looked back to the front," wrote Giles E. Wright in *The Blood-Horse*, "Porterhouse began his big move. When Shoe looked around the second time, Porterhouse's head already was nodding alongside Swaps' quarters, and Shoe went to work in a hurry."

Whip and scrub though he might, Shoemaker was unable to get Swaps to regenerate enough speed to stave off the bid of Porterhouse, whom Ismael (Milo) Valenzuela got rolling fast while in receipt of nine pounds from the favorite.

Five-year-old Porterhouse, who would retire to stud the winner of ten major sprint stakes, had been entered by Charlie Whittingham to ensure a lively pace for stablemate Mister Gus, who wound up third, five lengths behind Swaps.

Winner of the Futurity at Belmont as a juvenile, Porterhouse had been co-highweighted on the Experimental Free Handicap with Turn-to and at one time had been favored for the Kentucky Derby.

Porterhouse and Mister Gus were owned by the Llangollen Farm of Mary Elizabeth Whitney Lunn. She had just bought a ranch across the street from Ellsworth in Chino, owned some breeding stock in partnership with the cowboy, and stood Endeavour II at his ranch. She was one of Swaps' greatest fans.

Before the race Ellsworth and Tenney told some writers in the paddock that they were worried about Swaps being fit enough for the race because his sore foot had made it difficult to train him properly.

Whittingham, interviewed before the Californian, told a writer, "We have a couple of hickory-tough horses. We'll be in somebody's way out there."

Shoemaker readily accepted blame for the loss. "It wasn't his fault that he didn't win," he said. "I went to the front easily. He was just galloping along, pricking his ears in the stretch, and I eased up on him. When I saw the other horse coming, I couldn't get him to running again in time to hold him off."

Fans roundly booed the rider upon his return to the scales. They even booed him when he returned to the track for the next race, in which the rider's mount broke down on the backstretch to end a perfectly miserable day for the legendary reinsman.

Shoemaker later wrote that Tenney had told him before the Californian that Swaps was not dead fit and not to give him a hard race. The rider refuted the notion he had been caught napping. "I heard Porterhouse coming," he said. But he used his best judgment in trying to bring back a sound horse by not compromising his future on the day.

Ellsworth and Tenney took the loss like the sportsmen they were.

"Let's give Porterhouse and Charlie Whittingham and Mrs. Lunn the credit that is due them for the victory," Tenney said. "Porterhouse ran an excellent race. We were beaten by a real top horse."

Ellsworth said, "Anybody can make a mistake."

SWAPS

CHAPTER 10

"The greatest"

S waps may have lost the battle when ingloriously nailed in the Californian Stakes, but the fitness he gained in that infamous effort provided him with the strength to win the war of 1956. For in his next five starts at Hollywood Park, not only did the mighty chestnut triumph in all of his contests, he went on a record spree the likes of which have never been seen. He won each race in record time.

Tenney's task was not made miraculously simpler by Swaps having gotten dead fit in the Californian. It was not as if the statuesque idol had somehow been dipped in holy water and rendered free of any physical ailments.

In the two weeks between the ignoble defeat in the Californian and his impending engagement in the Argonaut Handicap, Swaps presented Tenney with a bruised bulb on the back of the notorious right front foot and a severe case of cracked heels.

"When a foot is not healthy," explained Dr. Jock Jocoy, "it doesn't just affect the foot alone, but the heels above it, the pastern, and even the ankle. We were always dealing not just with the foot, but other parts of that leg, too."

Rival horsemen noted that some of the methods Tenney used to care for the assorted foot and leg ailments were out of the norm. These so-called "cowboy" methods fell into what Tenney and Ellsworth proudly referred to as the "Arizona Method."

Whatever these tricks of the range were, they worked well enough for Swaps to make every dance through a demanding schedule at the lucrative spring/summer meeting. Tenney ran a stable for Ellsworth whose *raison d'être* was to make money. It was not a sporting venture, but a business. A horse such as Swaps had the potential to carry the entire stable. It was incumbent upon Tenney to have Swaps ready to dance all of the dances.

Tenney put the leather pad back on Swaps' foot for the Argonaut.

Swaps was assigned the top weight of 128 pounds for the one-mile Argonaut around two turns. He gave five pounds to Bobby Brocato, nine to Porterhouse, and thirteen to Poona II.

Bettors hammered the favorite down to odds of twenty cents on the dollar.

From the rail post Shoemaker broke just inside of Bobby Brocato, whose renowned front-running jockey, Johnny Longden, changed tactics. Shoemaker, realizing the situation, sent Swaps to the front to make his own pace, as Longden followed him, just in advance of Poona II. Porterhouse, a late-running sprinter, had trouble keeping up in fourth place.

Swaps sped through early splits of :22 2/5 and :45 1/5. Both Swaps and Bobby Brocato raced in hand through the devilishly fast early fractions. Longden asked his mount for his lick in the middle of the far turn, and Bobby Brocato ran up just past the middle of Swaps' body as they reached the three-quarters in 1:08 4/5.

Swaps stalled momentarily and pricked his ears as he spotted the starting gate just inside the final furlong. Shoemaker hit him to get his mind back on business. Shoemaker did not hit Swaps again but did wave the

stick beside the colt's head.

Swaps won in hand by a length and a quarter, with Bobby Brocato, in a game effort, reporting home six lengths in front of Porterhouse. The final time of 1:33 1/5 shattered the previous track record of 1:34 4/5 and lowered Citation's 1950 world record by two-fifths of a second.

While many among the crowd of 52,787 stared at the new record time lit up on the infield tote board and others in the winner's circle ceremony were caught up in the excitement of the moment, track photographer Vic Stein captured Ellsworth and Tenney focusing their gazes on Swaps' right front foot.

Tenney and Ellsworth both had predicted a world record in the paddock. After the race, Ellsworth reminded writers that, "Citation had a very fast pace-setter in Bolero. I believe that if Bobby Brocato had set the pace, Swaps could have run under 1:33."

Legitimacy of the record was brought into question by newspaper writers because of the obvious nature of a lightning-fast Hollywood Park strip that saw Colonel Mack run a mile and one-sixteenth in 1:41 and Bold Bazooka sprint three-quarters in 1:09 2/5 earlier on the card.

More than one veteran observer noted that the Golden Gate Fields surface the day Citation ran 1:33 3/5 had been plenty fast as well.

Swaps once again rekindled Westerners' pride in their hero. Now that Swaps was back in the winning column, local Turf writers once again began to fan the flames of regional rivalry.

Giving them some ammunition, Ellsworth in his first post-match comment for public consumption talked differently about the Washington Park race, saying, "We should never have run Swaps in that race with his bad foot. We debated three hours about it and finally went ahead with the race against our better judgment."

Westerners began to write that the connections of Nashua, once so eager to face Swaps, now were ducking the Ellsworth colorbearer since the score had been evened and it was obvious that Swaps once again seemed invincible.

They may have come close to the truth, because the ownership of Nashua had changed since the previous summer, as William Woodward Jr., only thirty-five, had died in a bizarre accident in which his wife shot him when she reportedly mistook him for an intruder in the dark.

Nashua in the summer of 1956 ran as the property of a syndicate that had acquired the colt for a world-record price of $1,251,200 through a sealed-bid auction. Innovator and bold player Leslie B. Combs II of Spendthrift Farm in Lexington, Kentucky, formed the syndicate and managed the colt.

The new manager's goal was to protect and enhance the value of his group's substantial investment, not to provide competitive sporting matches for racing fans or media highlights for Turf writers.

The Argonaut marked the first time in Swaps' career that he had gone right to the front and stayed there in a race run around two turns. Tenney said the race supplanted Swaps' effort in the pre-Kentucky Derby Jefferson Purse as the Khaled colt's most scintillating performance.

"His race in the Argonaut required something, and it was really a great performance," Tenney said.

Perennial leading Southern California trainer Bill Molter, who saddled Bobby Brocato, said, "That Swaps is the greatest horse I've ever seen in my life."

Fourteen days later, Swaps and Bobby Brocato, as well as Mister Gus, Rejected, and Colonel Mack, among others, suited up for the Inglewood Handicap at a mile and one-sixteenth.

Weight assignments for the Inglewood had Swaps at 130 — up two pounds — and Bobby Brocato at 121 — down two pounds, for a difference of four pounds from the Argonaut two weeks earlier. Mister Gus at 115 pounds was in receipt of fifteen pounds from the top-weight.

Molter, with his charge set to get a significant nine-pound pull in the weights, this time instructed Longden to send Bobby Brocato in the $50,000-added handicap.

Bobby Brocato went to the front. Longden, though, tried to back up the pace by rating his mount. The initial quarter was run in a relatively moderate :23 1/5, with Swaps tracking about a length and a half back in second and Mister Gus a similar margin behind Swaps.

Shoemaker, always restraining Swaps, let his mount creep closer on the backstretch as he started to pressure Bobby Brocato. The half-mile fraction, reached in :46, was in line with the earlier fraction. Swaps was a length off the pacesetter.

Tenney rarely gave instructions to Shoemaker. Alarmed by seeing the colt set a fast pace in the Argonaut, Tenney made an exception before the Inglewood, asking The Shoe not to let Swaps show too much speed too early. Tenney believed that horses should be reserved early and asked to run late. He thought they stayed sounder this way. He trained all of his horses with this strategy in mind.

Swaps crept closer and closer to Bobby Brocato. Leaving the backstretch, Shoemaker let Swaps have a bit more rein, and the red machine responded by collaring, passing, and putting three lengths of daylight between him and the pacesetter.

Shoemaker, ever cognizant of Swaps' habit of looking for the starting gate in the lane, had his stick ready. He did not have to hit the colt this time, instead showing it to the horse a few times in midstretch. Swaps reached the sixteenth pole. The tote board registered an unprecedented clocking for the first mile of 1:32 3/5. The Shoe took a strong hold in the final 110 yards, and geared Swaps down to hit the wire in 1:39.

Swaps won by two and three-quarters lengths, with Mister Gus passing a tired Bobby Brocato for second, two lengths ahead of the pacesetter.

The final time shattered Swaps' own world and track record by one and two-fifths seconds. Time for a mile was three-fifths of a second faster than the world record for the distance he had set fourteen days earlier.

It may have been Swaps' greatest display of speed. The record was not lowered until Hoedown's Day beat it at Bay Meadows in 1983, when he carried eleven pounds less than Swaps' 130-pound impost. Although a mile and one-sixteenth is one of the most commonly run distances on the American calendar, no horse at a major track has ever approached the time of Swaps.

The usually unflappable Robert Hebert, a longtime California correspondent for *The Blood-Horse* and a leading metropolitan newspaper handicapper whose success was attributed to privately formulated speed ratings, wrote as follows: "Until the Inglewood, I had always regarded Citation — when he was a three-year-old — as the greatest horse I had ever seen. Swaps

made me change my mind. He's not one of racing's all-time greats: he is the greatest."

Rex Ellsworth told Hebert, "One day before we retire him, I'd like to really open up with Swaps just once. I'd like to see just how fast he really can run. If Bill (Shoemaker) ever really hits him, he'll take off like a thunderbolt." Ellsworth maintained that Swaps was a true whip horse, one that really responded positively to a good whack or two.

Hebert visited his *beau ideal* the morning after the record run and found him standing square on both front feet, while shifting the weight off one of his hind legs.

"When he does that," Tenney told him, "I know that front foot is all right. Because that puts all the weight on his front. He wouldn't do that for a long time."

Tenney said that the foot was sound again. "As a result, Swaps is much stronger now. I think that is the big reason why he is running so well now — he's stronger," Tenney said.

Three days after the world-record performance, Al Wesson's publicity office primed the pump, generating a news item that quoted Ellsworth as saying that Leslie

Combs had backed out of a $300,000 match race (with $100,000 to the loser) between Nashua and Swaps at Hollywood Park.

"I thought it was all set," Ellsworth was quoted as saying, "but he backed out. I went after him real good over the phone. I told him we might come East after him. He said, 'Well, we don't have to run.' I said, 'We'll chase you right into the Atlantic Ocean.' He said, 'We still don't have to run.' "

According to the story, Combs supposedly told Ellsworth, "It takes twenty pounds off a horse's form to come to the West Coast." Ellsworth retorted, "It costs them forty pounds heading East into that hot, humid weather."

The good sportsmanship Ellsworth had displayed following the match race loss began to erode and be replaced by a growing cynicism, as the California horseman, emboldened by his steed's magnificent record accomplishments, became frustrated in his attempts to frame an arena in which Swaps could re-establish his dominance over Nashua.

"I don't think they'll ever let Nashua meet this colt again," he said.

According to the news item, Combs said, "The sportsmen who form our syndicate purchased Nashua primarily for breeding purposes. The decision to keep Nashua on the Eastern Seaboard was made on the advice of trainer Fitzsimmons, whose sportsmanship requires no reaffirmation from us."

The quintessential Kentucky promoter, Combs had used all of his considerable charm to balance his desire to buy Swaps as a stallion prospect with his responsibility to the Nashua syndicate's substantial investment. Turning down Ellsworth's plea for a return match race, while at the same time trying to hustle him for his horse, was a monumental task, one that he ultimately failed to pull off.

An ailment that had surfaced unbeknownst to the public but not to rival horsemen was revealed by Tenney prior to Swaps' next engagement in the American Handicap run on the Fourth of July in 1956.

Several days prior to the Argonaut, Swaps developed cracked heels a few inches above the chronically sore right front foot. The condition had been treated aggressively and resolved itself.

However, three days before the American Handicap,

a raw spot appeared in the same area. Tenney stayed in Swaps' stall and worked on the cracked heel until he felt he had it under control. It was nearly midnight before he came out of the stall.

Tenney and Ellsworth admitted to having a couple of sleepless nights before they deemed Swaps was ready to contest the American.

Only four horses lined up against Swaps for the $100,000-added American, in which the colt was set to carry 130 pounds, the same package he would be asked to carry in the last six starts of his career.

At the time, prevailing opinion among the leading givers of weight held that 130 pounds should be the uppermost limit in any handicap race. These handicappers were employed by racetracks, whose business it was to showcase the best horses available.

The 130-pound ceiling guaranteed the top horses would participate, not duck a hefty assignment and shop for a lighter impost elsewhere. To ensure competitive contests, handicappers adjusted the spread by lowering the weights of the weaker horses in an effort to bring the horses together.

Purists and modernists concerned themselves with

this issue in print, on the air, and in conversation. It was among the most debated topics of the day.

Because of the "ceiling," Swaps now was asked to give Bobby Brocato fifteen pounds (an additional "spread" of six pounds since their last meeting and twelve since their first meeting of the year). Bobby Brocato, a couple of months earlier, had shouldered 124 pounds when he became only the second horse in history to add the San Juan Capistrano Handicap to an earlier victory in the Santa Anita Handicap.

The top weight also had to concede nineteen pounds to Mister Gus, who was dropped four pounds from his second-place finish the time before in the Inglewood Handicap. Mister Gus eventually left town to avoid racing against Swaps, and he accounted for the Woodward Stakes and Arlington Handicap.

Swaps won the American Handicap by one and three-quarters lengths over Mister Gus, with six lengths separating him from Bobby Brocato and eight more lengths back to Blue Volt. The winner wandered all over the track, going wide early as Bobby Brocato and Mister Gus alternated on the pace. Swaps also drifted in during the stretch run.

The Ellsworth colt put in a solid kick around the turn and won in hand, as had become his habit. Tenney reckoned the cracked heel, which evinced signs of bleeding in the winner's circle, might have been stinging the colt and surmised that was the reason Swaps ran erratically.

The final time for a mile and one-eighth of 1:46 4/5 equaled the world record, set by Alidon in the same race a year earlier under 116 pounds.

Tenney and Ellsworth were not as interested in another time mark as in getting their horse back in one piece. So a couple of days earlier, when the Horsemen's Benevolent and Protective Association pressured Hollywood Park into slowing down the racing surface, Swaps' owner and trainer backed them all the way.

Figures-oriented handicapper Hebert reported that the track had been slowed down considerably for the American, which made Swaps' performance all the more remarkable.

Shoemaker, Tenney, and Ellsworth all agreed that Swaps was not at his best in the American Handicap.

It must be taken as an indication of Swaps' enormous

talent that, while forced to concede gobs of weight when racing with a painful malady, his connections felt it necessary to make excuses for an historic world-record performance under less than ideal circumstances.

CHAPTER 11

California Comet

I n the sweltering summer of 1956, nothing in racing was hotter than Swaps. The hottest topic of discussion, especially east of California where Nashua's supporters were encamped, centered around whether Swaps actually ran as blazingly fast as his record-setting spree indicated or whether the Hollywood Park racing surface was responsible for all of the new speed marks.

Figures handicapper and veteran racing analyst Robert Hebert, writing in *The Blood-Horse* following Swaps' win in the American Handicap, said, "Up until last year this reporter had always felt that Hollywood Park's track had been something special — something that couldn't be touched by any other track.

"Then last year it suddenly became the fastest track in the country — instead of the best. It seemed that

Hollywood Park was out to corral every world record in the books, and it almost succeeded."

The year before, when Ellsworth's homebred Khaled colt El Drag set a world record of 1:20 for seven furlongs at Hollywood Park, *Los Angeles Times* Turf scribe Paul Lowry wrote: "It seemed logical to question Tony Hanson about the speed of the Hollywood Park racing strip."

Track superintendent Hanson said, "Our track needs warmth to be at its best and make it move."

Lowry pressed Hanson to explain what he meant by "make it move."

"Well, it's live," said Hanson. "There are bacteria in it, and the track moves when the sun beats on it. The cushion becomes fluffier and better for horses."

Lowry asked Hanson what he put in the ground to create bacteria.

"That's a trade secret," Hanson said. "That's the only thing I've got."

By the middle of the Hollywood Park meeting a year later, horsemen had experienced about as much of Hanson's miracle racing surface as they were willing to take. Three out of four of them complained enough to George W. Ring, the California Horsemen's Benevolent and Protective Association division president, that he felt compelled to meet with Hollywood Park's management.

"For the first four weeks of the season," Ring said, "the Hollywood Park track was the finest in America. Then it got progressively harder and faster, and we had many complaints from trainers that their horses were going sore. There was trouble filling races because so many horses were sore. It was the same situation as last summer all over again."

By most accounts, Ring was successful in getting management to slow down the track. Hebert, as well as other metropolitan newspaper handicappers who used their own speed figures, concurred that prior to the American the track had been slowed down.

When Swaps ran his world-record 1:33 1/5 mile in the Argonaut to launch his summer of speed, Hebert in *The Blood-Horse* referenced his earlier notation that Hollywood Park had "tightened" the racing surface for the race, but following the colt's fast new standard in the Inglewood Handicap he wrote, "We should add here that the speed of the track was not changed for the Inglewood. It still is a fast track — perhaps the fastest in America — but the point is that it has remained constant. If it seemed abnormally fast for the Inglewood, Swaps made it look that way."

The one aspect of Swaps' assault on the record books that made it difficult for many Easterners to swallow was the ease with which the California horse was routinely piling up milestones.

Whitney Tower, who covered racing for the fledgling weekly magazine *Sports Illustrated*, was regarded as a Turf writer with an Eastern bent. By the middle of the season in 1956, however, Tower became a Swaps believer.

After witnessing Swaps equal the world record in the American Handicap, Tower cut the legs off the story that credited the California racing surface as the reason the colt had been able to run the record times by writing "the Hollywood Park strip with its three-inch cushion was no more like the proverbial pasteboard than any number of Eastern tracks I've seen."

As was the custom in the 1950s, weights for the Hollywood Gold Cup were released forty-five days before the race. The 130-pound assignment given to Swaps not only was covered by the racing journals, but was written about in general sports columns in the nation's newspapers.

A great debate took place in the mid 1950s between racing purists, who insisted that greatness in a racehorse could only be attained by carrying huge weight imposts, and racing secretaries, who tried to get by with a 130-pound ceiling in an effort to keep top horses from leaving town to race where they would receive lower weights.

Swaps drew attention to Hollywood Park like no horse before him, and the track's racing officials were not about to weight him out of making appearances.

"A handicapper should be free to call the weights as he sees them, without reference to the business office or the limits announced by any owner," Joe Estes wrote in *The Blood-Horse*, pointing a finger both at his friend Ellsworth and Hollywood Park.

Countering that argument in an address before a National Press Club meeting in Washington, D.C., Eddie Arcaro said, "You may ask why 130 pounds should be the limit. I can only tell you that it seems to be the breaking point."

Hollywood Park would distribute $162,000, the greatest amount ever paid by an association, for the Gold Cup. The winner would get $102,100 and the winning breeder an additional $10,000.

Mish Tenney, normally a sound sleeper, was restless the day before the Gold Cup. Awake at 1:30 Friday morning, he lay in bed wondering how Swaps was standing in his stall, whether the colt was shifting his body weight to rest his front feet.

The trainer got in his Oldsmobile, took the sixty-minute drive to Hollywood Park, several hours before usual, and found Swaps standing with his weight evenly distributed and not favoring his right front foot. Tenney then finished his night's sleep in his tack room.

More than 55,000 fans showed up for the Gold Cup. Nashua won the Monmouth Handicap that day, and news of the race, when intoned by track announcer Hal Moore, drew fewer boos and less applause than similar reports had generated earlier in the season.

West Coast racegoers and analysts, buoyed by the ease with which their hero had been mastering his opposition, had already concluded that Swaps was better than Nashua. Some now wondered whether Mister Gus couldn't handle the Belair Stud colt.

Once again Hollywood Park's fear of a minus pool and consequently a loss of revenue saw the track offer only win betting on the mile and one-quarter Gold Cup. The crowd sent off Swaps as the heavy choice at fifteen cents on the dollar, his lowest odds since paying $2.10 to win the previous season's Westerner against three-year-olds.

Swaps broke like lightning in the Gold Cup. Mindful of Tenney's desire to have his colt go as slowly as possible in the early running, Shoemaker had to reel in Swaps. Mister Gus went by him as the field passed the stands for the first time. Swaps was tractable through fractions of :23 and :45 2/5.

After the field reached the backstretch, Swaps crept closer, applying some heat to Mister Gus, who reached the three-quarters in 1:09. As was his style, Swaps went after the pacesetter around the turn.

"When I asked him for it on the far turn, he moved so easily that I actually had to take another hold to keep him back," Shoemaker said.

Swaps was in front with a mile in 1:33 1/5. Shoemaker waved the stick in front of the colt's eyes to mid-stretch, where Swaps built up a lead of more than four lengths. He was taken in hand near the end and won easily by two lengths over Mister Gus, who got thirteen pounds, with Porterhouse one and a quarter lengths farther away under 119 pounds.

The final time of 1:58 3/5 shattered Rejected's year-old track record by a full second and had been bettered in racing history only by Noor's 1:58 1/5 in 1950 at Golden Gate Fields.

Swaps emerged from the Gold Cup basically unscathed, with his right fore foot none the worse for wear and his cracked heel only mildly irritated. Ellsworth knew he had a license to print money and decided to wheel Swaps back in eleven days for the hundred-grand Sunset Handicap.

The Sunset was a handicap in title only. With Hollywood Park sticking to its 130-pound weight ceiling, Swaps was assured of not having to face any meaningful competition, because the spread made the imposts so low that horses such as Liz Whitney Lunn's Mister Gus and Porterhouse could not get a capable rider able to do the light weight. Mrs. Lunn refused to run either of her handicap stars.

Eight horses lined up against Swaps. All eight riders weighed more than their scheduled assignment. As an example, if a horse had been slated to carry 100 pounds, but the rider weighed 105, the horse was forced to carry five pounds extra weight.

Two riders carried five pounds extra and one toted four pounds extra. Since the actual differences between Swaps and his rivals was considerably less than had been assigned by the racing secretary, the effect of the "handicap" was to favor Swaps. The actual weight carried by the challengers ranged from 109 to 104 pounds.

Swaps would make such a mockery of the 130-pound ceiling on handicaps that its inventors, the year after Swaps retired from racing, abandoned the entire concept.

More of a coronation than a contest, the Sunset allowed the admirers of Swaps one last chance to see him perform in his native state. The big colt had reached the height of his physical powers, and Shoemaker had to use all of his strength to exert some control over the 1-10 favorite when the field was sent away on its one and five-eighths-mile journey.

With Shoemaker's feet high up on the dashboard in order to give the diminutive rider the most leverage possible, Swaps settled into a leisurely pace, as he maintained about a one and a half-length lead through splits of :23, :46 3/5, 1:11, 1:36 1/5, and 2:00 3/5.

Shoemaker let Swaps run about a furlong in the lat-

ter part of the race, and the colt opened by six lengths. The Shoe had the colt wrapped up as tightly as possible as he eased Swaps through the final sixteenth of a mile.

"He's like a mechanical rabbit the dogs can never catch," said Mel Peterson, who rode third-place finisher Blue Volt.

Bob Benoit descended the press box to get a quote from Shoemaker. "It was five minutes after the race," Benoit said, "and Shoe still couldn't uncurl his hands they hurt so much."

Swaps won the Sunset by four and a quarter lengths over Honey's Alibi. The final time of 2:38 1/5 lopped off two and two-fifths seconds from the Hollywood Park track record set the previous year by Social Outcast and one and three-fifths seconds from the world record set in 1949 when Ace Admiral won the Sunset the year it was run at Santa Anita because of a fire at Hollywood Park.

En route to the record clocking, Swaps reached one and one-half miles in 2:25 4/5, which was one and four-fifths seconds faster than the world mark, and one and three-eighths miles in 2:13 1/5, which was a second faster than the hitherto unapproachable thirty-five-year-old world mark set by Man o' War.

Dick Nash, a track-and-field filbert and racing statistician who directed publicity at Santa Anita, reported that not since Man o' War held five American records at the same time in 1920 had a racehorse compiled such a dossier of speed as Swaps.

The count of records, both world and American, for Swaps reached six with the Sunset result. The California Comet now held outright the world record on dirt for a mile, a mile and seventy yards, one and one-sixteenth miles, and one and five-eighths miles; a share of the world record for one and one-eighth miles on dirt; and a share of the American record for one and three-sixteenths miles on grass.

Swaps was transported the following day to Chicago. The day he arrived, Mister Gus took two-fifths of a second off Swaps' American record for one and three-sixteenths miles on turf and validated Western form by carrying 118 pounds to victory in the $154,850 Arlington Handicap over such handicap stalwarts as Summer Tan and Fisherman.

Mister Gus, prior to invading Chicago, had been in receipt of nine, fifteen, nineteen, and thirteen pounds from Swaps in California. He would go on to defeat

Nashua in the Woodward Stakes in New York under weight-for-age conditions.

Western pride reached a fever pitch after the Sunset. Hollywood Park announcer Moore kicked off the proceedings as Swaps entered the winner's circle by announcing that the chestnut colt was "perhaps the greatest horse that ever lived."

A commentary recapping the Sunset for *The Thoroughbred of California* summed up the mood. "We in the West are often derided for our fierce and sometimes foolish sectional loyalty. The derision comes, of course, from equally fervent praise shouters who favor the Ivy League and mint julep set beyond the Mississippi. The only reason that they out-yell, out-sneer and out-vote us is that there are more of them."

The later success of Mister Gus against Nashua would serve only to underscore the emptiness experienced by the Swaps' camp and racing fans across the nation in not being able to see another match race between Swaps and Nashua. Westerners became convinced more than ever that Swaps would reverse the previous match race result.

SWAPS

CHAPTER 12

In The Balance

M ister Gus traveled on an airplane from Hollywood Park to Arlington Park for his record-breaking victory in the summer of 1956. He arrived fresh, and two days later lowered Swaps' American record. When Swaps went to Chicago, he rode the rails.

Mish Tenney of the "Arizona Method" preferred to ship by van or railroad car. He thought horses arrived in better condition when they could travel, head to tail, at a steady pace. Tenney himself enjoyed riding the rails. In fact, prior to leaving for the match race a year earlier, the trainer had invited a few of his friends in the media to join the fun and share in the camaraderie on the *Santa Fe Chief*.

About three weeks after arriving in Chicago, Swaps was 3-10 to beat seven rivals on turf in the $50,000 Arch Ward Memorial Handicap, on the same course and at the same distance over which he had won the previous summer's American Derby at Washington Park in American record time.

Swaps carried his now customary 130 pounds, and he was set to concede from fourteen to twenty-seven pounds.

Swaps tracked pacesetter Howdy Baby early, moved into contention down the backstretch, engaged the new leader Sir Tribal on the stretch curve, then steadily fell back to finish next to last, beaten about six lengths.

The seventh-place finish would be the worst of Swaps' career and marked only the second time in twenty-five outings that he failed to finish in the top three. He had been fifth in his fifth outing at two in the C.S. Howard Stakes.

The course was labeled "firm," and the final time was only two-fifths of a second slower than the course record Swaps had set a year earlier, but Bill Shoemaker said, "Swaps just couldn't take to the grass. It was too soft for him, and he labored all the way up the backstretch."

According to Rex Ellsworth, "You could just see he wasn't right. He had lost about seventy pounds. He just wasn't feeling good."

Regardless of how less robust Swaps had appeared to

Ellsworth and how underachieving his performance had been to Shoemaker, Tenney once again brought the horse back in quick order, this time in nine days, for the Labor Day renewal of the Washington Park Handicap, a one-mile event on the main track.

The crowd of 40,073 — the largest to see a horse race in Chicago since 1946 — let Swaps get away at forty cents on the dollar, the most generous odds offered on the red colt since his February comeback race. With the 130-pound package in place aboard the favorite, five lined up against Swaps, including 115-pound second top-weight Summer Tan. Sea o Erin got eighteen pounds; Sir Tribal, sixteen; and Hasseyampa and Dogoon, eighteen each.

Summer Tan set the pace and held a daylight lead through sizzling fractions on the straightaway of :22 1/5 and :44 1/5. He put away Dogoon early. Swaps tracked in third, moved to Summer Tan around the turn, and was in front turning for home. The three-quarters in 1:07 4/5 belonged to Swaps.

Swaps opened up at will in mid-stretch, building a commanding lead of more than three lengths. He won by two lengths, with his ears pricked and Shoemaker having him firmly in hand.

The official chart of the race noted: Swaps "was fairly well in hand all through the last seventy yards." Shoemaker said the colt won with authority, but that he had him "doing his best" in the end. Most press reports mirrored the view of the *Daily Racing Form*'s trackman. The Shoe may have been posturing with Eastern Seaboard racing secretaries in mind.

The first-prize money of $88,750 from the $142,700 purse increased the colt's earnings to $848,900 and brought his career race record in twenty-five outings to nineteen wins, two seconds, and two thirds.

The final time of 1:33 2/5 shaved two-fifths of a second from the track record set five years earlier by Bernwood under 116 pounds. Once again Swaps had run in record time while finishing in hand. It was the ninth time the California speedster had run in at least track- or course-record time. It was the tenth time in his last fourteen starts that he had run in record time. It was the third time Swaps had run in record time outside the Golden State.

Three days after the Washington Park Handicap, Rex Ellsworth told the press he had sold a half-interest in Swaps to John W. Galbreath, the Ohio-based residential and commercial real estate developer who owned Darby Dan Farm in Lexington, Kentucky, as well as the Pittsburgh Pirates baseball club.

Darby Dan originally had been the centerpiece of historic Idle Hour Stock Farm on Old Frankfort Pike, where Colonel Edward Riley Bradley bred and raised five Kentucky Derby winners. Galbreath and his wife, Dorothy (who owned Summer Tan in her own name), had developed one of the better stallion rosters in the Bluegrass and would one day stand Swaps' contemporary Ribot, the unbeaten two-time Prix de l'Arc de Triomphe hero held by Europeans to be Swaps' superior.

Ellsworth reported that Galbreath had agreed to pay one million dollars in cash and bloodstock to acquire the fifty-percent interest. Ellsworth said he sold the interest because he had no more than ten mares free of Khaled blood that were good enough to be bred to Swaps.

The acquisition by Galbreath was not reported to the press until a few days after Swaps had won the Washington Park Handicap. Tommy Bell has a different version.

"Galbreath wanted to buy Swaps," said the son of high-profile bloodstock agent Ray Bell, "but Rex didn't want to sell. Said the horse would be an annuity for his family.

"My father, Ellwood Johnston, and Rex decided to go to the Keeneland sales. They drove down there in my father's car. All the way down there they worked on Rex, trying to get him to sell."

Ellsworth did not immediately concede. While in Lexington for the yearling sale, which was held late that summer, Ellsworth talked further with Nashua's syndicator, Leslie B. Combs II of Spendthrift Farm, about a possible deal on Swaps. Nothing came of their meetings because of Ellsworth's reluctance to sell all of his interest in Swaps.

Combs said, "I had first refusal on buying the horse as a whole. I've been successful with handling stallions through syndication, which involved managing them myself." Combs also wanted Swaps to stand in 1957, and Ellsworth wanted to prolong his racing career.

Tommy Bell, whose father had brokered a deal several years earlier that allowed Ellsworth to obtain breeding seasons in stallions owned by Louis B. Mayer by trading cattle, said, "Finally, Rex told my father he'd sell half of Swaps. 'Bring your man on,' he said.

"I was at Washington Park at the time. So we went down to Midway Airport in Chicago and picked up Mr.

and Mrs. Galbreath. They came in on their private plane. I drove them to Washington Park. Rex had a trailer there. They all went into the trailer and hammered out a deal.

"After it was over, my dad said, 'Look, Rex, Mr. Galbreath has just shook hands with you to buy this horse; he's running this afternoon in the Arch Ward Handicap, maybe he'd like to see him.

"So we went over there. Old Josie, the Hungarian groom, was across the street having a beer. There wasn't a soul in the barn.

"There was Swaps, in the corner of the stall, eating chopped alfalfa. The horse was going to run in an hour and a half! Rex goes into the stall. Didn't even put a halter on the horse. Got him to stand up there. Man, he looked beautiful. Mr. Galbreath fell in love with the horse.

"So now he runs in the afternoon. Swaps ran the worst race he ever ran in his life. While leaving the track, getting ready to drive Mr. and Mrs. Galbreath back to the airport, Dad whispers to me while we're walking in front, 'There goes our deal.' So halfway to the airport, Mr. Galbreath turns to Dad and says, 'Rex won't back out on me will he?' "

If Bell's recollection is accurate, perhaps news of the sale was not released after the dismal Arch Ward effort in order to wait for a more opportune time, such as after a track-record win in the Washington Park Handicap.

One condition of the deal called for Swaps to stand initially at the Ellsworth Ranch in Chino, the next year at Darby Dan under the supervision of former key Bradley adviser Olin Gentry, and alternate each year afterward. Swaps would race as long as it was deemed advisable, and no date was set for his retirement. Galbreath's colors reportedly would be carried by his new acquisition.

Swaps never ran again.

An intended start in the September 15 United Nations Handicap was scrapped on race day when Tenney was unable to relieve pressure that had built up in the colt's right fore foot and that failed to respond to resetting of the shoe.

Ellsworth accepted an invitation to run November 12 in the International at Laurel Park. Breezing seven-eighths on October 9 at Garden State Park, where Tenney had moved his stable, Swaps took a bad step.

Although somebody nearby on a pony heard a noise "like the snap of a pistol," an initial set of X-rays revealed nothing.

A second set of X-rays the next morning showed two non-displaced fractures on the left hind leg about two inches in length. A light protective cast was placed on the leg and a cautiously optimistic diagnosis was proffered.

However, in struggling to get to his feet five days later, Swaps struck the injured leg against the side of his stall, breaking the cast and lengthening the fracture line into the joint below.

George Palmer Jr., the stable's veterinarian, and Jacques Jenney, a bone specialist from the veterinary school at the University of Pennsylvania, rigged a sturdier, more severe cast, one supported by long u-shaped metal bars that extended vertically from one side of the hock to the other and looped the foot.

Nashua's octogenarian trainer "Sunny Jim" Fitzsimmons, hearing of the injury, phoned Tenney and graciously offered a belly sling he had used successfully years before on a horse of his with a broken leg. Fitzsimmons sent over the sling, which gave Swaps the ability to shift his weight off the injured leg.

Swaps' life literally hung in the balance as he rested in the sling. Such was Tenney's concern over the well being of his beloved colt that the trainer did not leave his prized pupil's side during the first thirty-six hours and stayed on for eighteen days, after which Reed Ellsworth, one of Rex's brothers, picked up the vigil.

Forty-nine days after breaking his leg, Swaps was able to support himself without the sling. He was flown to California on December 9. When the DC6A cargo plane landed at Burbank Airport north of Hollywood, some two hundred people were on hand to greet him, amid newsreel floodlights and popping flashbulbs from newspaper photographers' cameras.

The singular nature of his temperament, as evidenced by a completely serene composure, allowed Swaps to survive the aftermath of an injury complication that would have spelled the end of most horses. He even gave his owner-breeder the hope of seeing him run again.

SWAPS

CHAPTER 13

Something To See

S waps survived his close brush with death in great part because of a placid emotional make-up, which was reflected in his remarkable disposition.

The week of the 1956 Hollywood Gold Cup, when Swaps was at the height of his powers as a racehorse, offered some examples of his gentle nature.

On big race days, cowboy friends of Ellsworth and Tenney would arrive at the track to watch Swaps run. The morning of the Gold Cup, a bunch of these cowpokes showed up at the barn.

"Mish was awful proud of Swaps," recalled stable veterinarian Jock Jocoy. "So he took a few of his friends into Swaps' stall to show him off. Well, after a minute or so, these cowboys — you know how they can be — they started playing grab-ass, right in the stall.

"They're rolling around on the floor, and Swaps is

kind of dancing in place, you know how they do, just sort of stepping to avoid the cowboys. The horseplay didn't faze the colt at all."

The morning after the Gold Cup, Hollywood Park publicist Bob Benoit stopped by the Ellsworth barn to ask Tenney how Swaps had come out of the race.

"He was talking with a girl in a wheelchair," Benoit said. "She was a fan of Swaps. They were at the bottom of the shed row, and she asked if she could see Swaps. Tenney had the webbing opened in front of Swaps' stall, and he told Swaps to come down the aisle toward them.

"Swaps had nothing on, no bridle, no halter — nothing. Using only verbal commands, Tenney had Swaps come down the ramp. He then put the wheelchair next to the horse. The girl's mother took a snapshot. Tenney then slapped Swaps on the rump, and the horse went right back into his stall. It was the most amazing thing I ever saw."

Four days before the Gold Cup, motion-picture director David Butler turned barn 57 into a set for a movie featuring former child star Margaret O'Brien in her first adult role.

Amid the glare of klieg lights, the shouts of workers,

and the bulkiness of the cameras, Tenney delighted in the action. "Well, Dave Butler knows that we don't get upset about such things, in fact, rather welcome them, so that is why he chose our barn. Actually it will do Swaps a lot of good, for we like him to be around activity," Tenney said.

Miss O'Brien asked if it would be possible for her to ride Swaps. Tenney obliged at once, and the actress rode the world's most valuable piece of horseflesh around the tow ring for ten minutes.

Although these circumstances admittedly were of a special nature, Tenney's regular morning routine included having Chester White walk Swaps over to the rail after his morning exercise and allow fans to pet him.

"The Rex Ellsworth colt and his trainer, Meshach Tenney, are an answer to a press-agent's prayer," Frank E. Butzow wrote in *The Blood-Horse* after the Westerners invaded Chicago for the match race in the summer of 1955. "They literally stand for almost anything. The word 'stand' is used advisedly. One of the best-mannered three-year-olds which could be found, Swaps poses for photographers as expertly as if he had earned all of his $328,950 that way."

The morning after the 1955 Kentucky Derby, Lexington-based equine artist Allen F. Brewer Jr. stopped by Tenney's barn at Churchill Downs and asked Ellsworth if he could take a conformation photograph of Swaps.

The colt was led out, and Brewer went to take his picture. Ellsworth interceded, saying the horse could stand better. Tenney adjusted the colt's stance by moving a fore leg and pulling back a hind leg.

"The horse stood in that position for eighteen minutes without moving a leg," said Brewer.

Writing in *The Blood-Horse*, Joe Estes, in a report of the 1955 Kentucky Derby, noted, "Nearly everyone who had anything to do with Swaps the two weeks he was in Louisville was impressed with the horse's gentleness, patience, and good behavior. He worked when he was supposed to, clowned when he was allowed to, and relaxed when he felt like it. In all, his bearing was that of a well-trained, well-conditioned athlete."

Swaps' attitude allowed him to develop his athletic gifts to their fullest. Great athletes, whether human or equine, achieve their greatest marks when they relax sufficiently to allow their speed to be fully realized.

By many accounts, this athleticism and, more specifically, his stride were the keys to Swaps' records.

Charles Hatton, before the match race, wrote in *Daily Racing Form*, "Swaps' temperament is singularly sweet...But it is in action that the champion of the Derby is seen to best advantage. He is a particularly alert post horse and has a low, stealthy manner of going once on stride, seeming to float along with the minimum of lost motion.

"His head is carried neither too high nor too low, and he has the facility for lengthening and accelerating his stride without appearing to exert himself at all.

"Swaps is one of the few horses, like Tom Fool, who sometimes are photographed in action with both forefeet extended as medieval artists used to depict the champions of the English turf. It is a distinctive peculiarity of gait which must be seen to be believed and one often hears visitors to equine art exhibitions question if ever a horse 'runs like that' at any phase of his stride."

Perhaps Hatton summed up the magical nature of the subject's mastery over all he surveyed in the West and the skepticism of the Eastern critics best, when he

wrote: "Swaps at times appeared almost to achieve levitation over the 'pasteboard' surfaces."

When Swaps went on his record-breaking spree at four, much talk followed about what made his stride so special. Ace Hollywood Park publicist Al Wesson on the eve of the 1956 Hollywood Gold Cup generated a news release on the subject, revealing that track super Tony Hanson had dispatched a crew manned with steel tapes to measure Swaps' stride after the American Handicap.

"The measurements were taken on the turn for home between the five-sixteenths and quarter pole," wrote Wesson. "It was during this sixteenth of a mile that Swaps was making a strong move and passing Mister Gus and Bobby Brocato on the outside.

"At the five-sixteenths Swaps' stride was 22'10". As he flew by his opponents it increased inch by inch to 23'3" which he held for five strides except for one at 23'4".

Presented with these details, Tenney remarked that "length of stride is not a particularly important item." What counted, he said, is "the quickness, smoothness and ease with which he gathers for the next stride. When the strides come easily and apparently effortlessly, that's more important than how long they are.

"I don't know whether Swaps' stride is average, long, or short. I do know, though, that Rex Ellsworth and I like the way he takes them."

Shoemaker said he could tell when Swaps was running fast because he could "feel the effort."

"He had a longer stride than most horses, but he had it together," explained The Shoe. "He wasn't one of those big, plodding, long-striding horses. He ran like a sprinter — quick and speedy and shifty."

B.K. Beckwith, an author and equine historian who saw Man o' War and Swaps race, said, "Man o' War had a longer stride (than Swaps), but both of them ran with an easy, flowing motion."

Dirt tracks in the West have always been faster than the sand tracks in the East. And because of it, Westerners learned to love speed. Fans in California came to idolize Swaps because when he ran faster than any other horse in history, he did it with such ease.

It would be difficult for anybody not living in Southern California at the time to appreciate the importance Swaps had on the sports scene in the West. Union Oil Company produced a color photograph of Swaps (taken by famous equine cinematographer Joe

Burnham) suitable for framing that was quickly gob-
bled up by fans hungry for tributes to their idol.

A few days prior to the 1955 Westerner Stakes,
Hollywood Park ran a newspaper ad, in which a pen-
ciled head study of Swaps was followed by a first-
person story by the horse and an invitation for fans to
request a copy of the ad. By the weekend Hollywood
Park had received almost five thousand letters.

Mervyn LeRoy announced in the summer of 1956
that Hollywood Park would commission "the best
sculptor available" to depict Swaps. Two years later, a
life-sized bronze of the colt, with all four feet off the
ground, was unveiled at the Inglewood track. The
Albert Stewart tribute hovers in the gardens of the
clubhouse entrance.

Swaps left two indelible marks on racing in the
West. He revitalized business at the two major tracks by
widening the fan base. And, he legitimized the quality
of the sport.

Swaps in 1956 became the first California-bred in the
modern era to be voted Horse of the Year despite, as
Whitney Tower wrote in *Sports Illustrated*, "some hard
knocks of eastern critics who write off California perfor-

mances and times as just so much worthless hokum."

Leon Rasmussen, an unabashed advocate of Western racing, symbolized years of frustration when he wrote in *The Thoroughbred of California* that by being voted Horse of the Year, Swaps "swept away the stubborn traces of provincialism on the American turf."

In noting that "the birth of this poll (*Daily Racing Form* and *Morning Telegraph*) and the re-birth of California breeding spring from practically the same dates," Rasmussen proffered an opinion that "now that the break-through has been made (by California breeding), the future is limitless. Other California-breds to come will certainly emulate or approximate the record of the chestnut pathfinder."

In fact, Swaps was a freak, and his counterpart has never returned, at least not in California and maybe no place else. Forty-four seasons would pass before Tiznow in 2000 became the second California-bred to be selected Horse of the Year.

Swaps had an amazing season at four. His only losses came when Porterhouse sneaked up on him in the Californian as Shoemaker was easing him and when he failed to act on turf less than firm in the Arch Ward.

Otherwise, Swaps won his other eight races, all of them in hand, and all but his return in February in world-, American-, or track-record time. In the ensuing years, only Dr. Fager and Secretariat would rock the record books with such force.

American racing fans did not get to see the entire package opened in 1956. A return match between Swaps and Nashua never took place, in large part because Nashua's new ownership was understandably concerned with protecting its investment, and Tenney and Ellsworth never got a chance to give Swaps their intended send off.

"You know, Shoemaker never really opened up on this horse," said Tenney. "He was easing him in the closing stages of almost all his races. We had planned to have Swaps really run for time, perhaps in his last race. It would have been something to see."

CHAPTER 14

A Legend

D orothy Galbreath purchased Rex Ellsworth's remaining fifty-percent interest in Swaps in 1957. News that Summer Tan's owner had bought the remaining interest to join her husband in full ownership of the 1956 Horse of the Year was released to the media in the fall, a year after Galbreath purchased the initial half-interest.

As with the original purchase, which was concealed until the timing was deemed propitious, plenty of evidence suggests the second half-interest in Swaps actually had been acquired several months earlier.

Swaps had entered stud in the spring of 1957 at Ellsworth Ranch in Southern California. Ellsworth and the Galbreaths planned to breed a dozen mares each, about half the size of a normal book, until it could be determined that his surgically repaired hind leg could handle the stress associated with covering mares.

After Swaps' hind legs were determined to be sound, the partners decided to sell a few seasons to breeders such as Liz Whitney Lunn at a figure of $10,000, the highest advertised stud fee at the time.

John Galbreath and Olin Gentry, according to Tommy Bell, were aghast at the crude, unkempt Ellsworth Ranch that was set up like a cattle stockyard. Galbreath could not bear the thought of having to board his prized mares at the Chino facility, where Swaps was scheduled to stand in alternating seasons. International real estate magnate Galbreath was more used to his own Bluegrass showplace at Darby Dan Farm.

It was widely reported that the second half of Swaps was sold for one million dollars, money with which Ellsworth said he could increase his bloodstock holdings by allowing him to diversify his bloodlines.

After Swaps was sent from California to Darby Dan Farm for his second breeding season, Mrs. Galbreath's buyout of Ellsworth was announced, and the horse never returned to California.

Of all the horses born in 1952 that became stallions in North America, Swaps wound up as the second-most successful sire of his generation in terms of Average-

Earnings Index (AEI), a qualitative measurement of success based on the racetrack earnings of the offspring of a sire. *The Blood-Horse* editor Joe Estes, who helped Ellsworth evaluate Khaled, developed the rating.

Swaps' AEI of 2.15 placed him behind only his racetrack nemesis Nashua's 2.37. Swaps sired about eight percent stakes winners to foals.

Swaps' best racehorses came from his first three crops. The Galbreaths' Polynesian mare Banquet Bell produced two of them.

The first foal from the first crop of Swaps for the Galbreaths was Banquet Bell's daughter Primonetta, a filly with the same lovely head as her sire. She won the Alabama Stakes at Saratoga and the Delaware Oaks at three. After she won the Spinster Stakes at Keeneland at four, she was voted champion handicap mare.

Thoroughbred breeders monitor the success of new stallions with an eye toward using them when mating their mares. Breeders considered Swaps to be a sensation by the time his third crop of foals turned three in 1963.

From that crop (foals of 1960), Swaps was represented by two of the top Triple Crown prospects in the country as well as his most accomplished daughter.

Chateaugay, a Darby Dan Farm homebred, and No
Robbery, a Greentree Stud homebred, were the two
best classic candidates in the nation.

Chateaugay, a full brother to Primonetta, improved
after wind surgery at two to win the Kentucky Derby
and Belmont Stakes, as well as to finish second in the
Preakness (to Ellsworth's homebred Candy Spots). No
Robbery won the Wood Memorial in sensational fashion, but bucked his shins in the Kentucky Derby. He
never reached his full potential, even though he did
come back to win his only start at four.

Affectionately, a homebred for Ethel D. Jacobs
trained by husband Hirsch Jacobs, was the most brilliant foal ever sired by Swaps. Among her nine wins in
a championship season at two, she won the Spinaway
and Sorority stakes. She raced through age five, winning eighteen added-money events and was voted
champion handicap mare and champion sprinter as a
five-year-old.

Swaps reached the height of fashion in 1961 at a
time when his oldest foals raced at three. That summer
at Keeneland, Humphrey Finney on behalf of John M.
Olin bought a Swaps colt out of Obedient from Leslie

Combs II's Spendthrift Farm consignment for $130,000. This marked the first time a yearling in America made six figures and broke the world record of $118,400 established in 1945 in England for the purchase of subsequent Irish Derby hero Sayajirao. Olin's colt, named Swapson, fared poorly at the track.

Swaps did sire a few more quality runners among his thirty-five stakes winners, including a Kentucky Oaks winner in Lady Vi-E. However, he never replicated his early feats at stud.

Combs realized a long-held dream in 1967, when he bought Swaps and syndicated him at age fifteen for $20,000 a share to stand at Spendthrift Farm, where for five seasons he stood alongside Nashua.

Swaps' influence as a progenitor in modern-day pedigrees is found not through his sons but his daughters. Kentucky breeders considered Swaps to be a good sire of broodmares, and the evidence still backs up that opinion.

Swaps' most prominent accomplishment in today's top international pedigrees is as the sire of Soaring. She is the second dam of Ballade, who is responsible for Glorious Song (champion older mare), her full brothers Devil's Bag (champion colt at two and sire) and

Saint Ballado (sire), and her sons Rahy (sire) and Singspiel (Dubai World Cup).

Another place of prominence for Swaps is as the sire of Intriguing. She is the dam of Numbered Account (champion filly at two), who is responsible for Private Account (sire) and Polish Numbers (sire). Another daughter of Intriguing named Playmate is the dam of Woodman (champion colt at two in Ireland), sire of Timber Country (Preakness), Hansel (Preakness and Belmont Stakes), and Bosra Sham (champion filly at three in England).

Another important position occupied by Swaps in an international pedigree is as the sire of Change Water. She is the dam of Fall Aspen, a Broodmare of the Year who is the dam of nine stakes winners, including classic winner Timber Country and the dam of Dubai Millennium, considered by some to be the greatest European runner since Ribot.

Swaps' best distaffers on the track proved to be his best producers in the paddock. Primonetta gave Darby Dan Farm Cum Laude Laurie (Beldame), Maud Muller (Ashland), and Prince Thou Art (Florida Derby). Two of her sons, Grenfall and Truxton King, became useful sires.

Affectionately's first foal was Personality, who was
Horse of the Year and champion colt at three, the year
he won the Preakness, Wood Memorial, and
Woodward Stakes.

Daughters of Swaps have produced such important
runners, sires, and producers as Best Turn (sire),
Woodchopper (second to Pleasant Colony in the
Kentucky Derby), Alma North (Matchmaker),
Cheriepe (San Antonio), Agitate (Hollywood Derby),
and Maximova (Prix de la Salamandre).

Swaps was humanely destroyed on November 3,
1972, at age twenty, at Spendthrift Farm, where three
weeks earlier, due to a skeletal structure weakened by
crippling arthritis, he had fallen in his stall. That same
year five other winners of the Kentucky Derby expired,
including Iron Liege, the 1957 winner produced by
Swaps' second dam.

Swaps was many things to many different people.
To Rex Ellsworth, he was the embodiment of a lifelong
study in the pursuit of physical perfection in a
Thoroughbred. To Mesach Tenney, he was a once-in-a-
lifetime athlete. To Bill Shoemaker, if asked at the right
moment, he was the best horse he ever rode. To Mr.

and Mrs. John W. Galbreath, he was the key in opening the door to classic success. To his admirers, he was a joy to behold in full flight. To Nashua's fans, he was a thorn in the side. To a crippled girl in a wheelchair, he was a source of inspiration. To newcomers lured by television, he was the source of a lifelong addiction. To jaded newspapermen, he was the fastest horse since Man o' War. To the Eastern Establishment, he was perceived as a threat to an entire industry. To figures filberts, he still confounds with his dossier of high-octane performances. To California breeders, he was a source of pride. To those who came after his passing and read of him, he was a legend.

SWAPS

EPILOGUE

Faded But Not Forgotten

R ex Ellsworth was the leading owner and breeder in North America in 1962 and 1963, when his stable hit its zenith, campaigning homebreds Candy Spots (Preakness Stakes), Olden Times (Metropolitan Handicap), and Prove It (Santa Anita Handicap). Nobody ever questioned his ability to develop and select horses. His business acumen, however, proved his failing. Ellsworth was more interested in the next deal than in solidifying his gains. Ambitious undertakings, such as building a racetrack and sales complex to compete with Keeneland, left him financially vulnerable. Ironically, he embarked upon his great venture in Thoroughbreds when he bought his first draft of mares at auction on Paris Pike and met his demise in the failed racetrack-sales complex on the same thoroughfare, a journey separated by one and a half miles of road and three decades. An alliance with notorious Southern California financier C. Arnholt Smith, who went to jail for questionable banking practices, put Ellsworth on a thin financial plane. He never really recovered.

He reached rock bottom in January of 1975 when it was discovered that horses on his Chino property were not being fed because Ellsworth had not provided enough money to a son who managed the ranch. A cause célèbre ensued that received extensive media coverage, embarrassing not only Ellsworth, his family, and friends, but the California breeding and racing community. Ellsworth kept a low profile for several years, but then was seen occasionally at horse sales. Age had left his face leaner, but it served to accentuate even more the piercing and observant blue eyes that had been the key to his success. In one of his last public appearances, he presented a trophy to the winner of the Swaps Stakes at Hollywood Park in 1996. Ellsworth died in 1997 at age eighty-nine in Chino.

Mesach Tenney rose to the heights of the training profession in the early 1960s, when he seemed to have a virtual stranglehold on the California handicap ranks. As the quality of Ellsworth's horses diminished, Tenney became less able to produce important winners. When Ellsworth's family became more involved in the breaking and training of the horses, Tenney's role was reduced. The stable fell apart when Ellsworth's equine empire crumbled under the weight of risky financial dealings. By the time Tenney retired in 1973, he had become an afterthought on the California racing scene. He mounted a half-hearted comeback in the 1980s, which lasted only a short while, but did see him send out Fairly Old to take the Somethingroyal Handicap at Hollywood Park in 1987 to become stakes winner number thirty-six to be saddled by Tenney. He died in 1993 at the age of eighty-five in a Utah nursing home, two years after being inducted into racing's Hall of Fame.

Bill Shoemaker became the winningest rider of all time, passing Swaps' Santa Anita Derby pilot John Longden. He rode many of the greatest American racehorses from the 1950s through the 1980s. In addition to winning the Kentucky Derby on Swaps, he lost an infamous running when he misjudged the finish line on Gallant Man. He then made amends winning the Run for the Roses with Tomy Lee, Lucky Debonair, and Ferdinand (at age fifty-four in 1986). During most of his riding career, he was reluctant to single out the mount he considered the best. After riding Spectacular Bid, he named him as the best horse he had ever ridden, although this pronouncement may have had more to do with business pressures than athletic merit. Pressed one evening by a longtime friend, Shoemaker admitted that Swaps was the best. Inducted into the Hall of Fame in 1958, Shoemaker became a successful trainer in the 1990s in California. His career was compromised and eventually halted by the effects of a car accident, in which he drove off a freeway on-ramp while reportedly under the influence of alcohol. He later reached a settlement on his claim against the maker of the automobile. He lives in San Marino, California.

John W. Galbreath was able to achieve his first success in a Triple Crown race with a son of Swaps in Chateaugay, but it was not his last, as the master of Darby Dan won another Kentucky Derby with Proud Clarion, a Preakness and Belmont with Little Current, and an English Derby with Roberto. He developed Darby Dan into one of the premier stallion stations in the Bluegrass, at one time or another standing classic sires Ribot, Swaps, Roberto, Graustark, His Majesty,

Sea-Bird, and Sword Dancer. Among the last of an almost extinct breed, Galbreath bred privately for the classics and was considered one of the greatest sportsmen of the last century. He died in 1988 at age ninety-one. Darby Dan, operated by his heirs, continues to produce champion racehorses.

Leslie B. Combs II, credited with popularizing the syndication of stallions in America, vied with Claiborne Farm from the 1950s through the 1970s for leadership in standing the most successful sires in the country. A gifted horseman as well as a promoter extraordinaire, he syndicated and stood such classic sires as Raise a Native, Exclusive Native, Nashua, Never Bend, Seattle Slew, Caro, Prince John, and Turn-to. A leading breeder, Combs bred and sold Majestic Prince (Kentucky Derby and Preakness) and Mr. Prospector (leading sire). Breeding for the market, he sold the country's first six-figure yearling in Swapson and several times sold the top yearling at Keeneland in July. Against his better judgment, Combs joined his son Brownell in the mid-1980s to take Spendthrift Farm public, but a few years later a class-action lawsuit by investors caused the break up of the most successful and prominent

commercial breeding venture the Bluegrass had ever known. He died at age eighty-eight in 1990.

Swaps was inducted into the Hall of Fame in 1966, a year after the induction of his racetrack rival, Nashua.

Swaps' name was apropos, as Swaps changed venues often, not only during his lifetime, but afterward as well. Two weeks before Shoemaker piloted Ferdinand to win the 1986 Kentucky Derby, the remains of Swaps were transferred from Spendthrift Farm to a memorial garden adjacent to the Kentucky Derby Museum at Churchill Downs, where he is buried alongside Carry Back and Brokers Tip.

SWAPS'
PEDIGREE

KHALED, br, 1943	Hyperion, 1930	Gainsborough, 1915	Bayardo Rosedrop
		Selene, 1919	Chaucer Serenissima
	Eclair, 1930	Ethnarch, 1922	The Tetrarch Karenza
SWAPS, chestnut colt, 1952		Black Ray, 1919	Black Jester Lady Brilliant
	Beau Pere, 1927	Son-in-Law, 1911	Dark Ronald Mother-in-Law
		Cinna, 1917	Polymelus Baroness La Fleche
IRON REWARD, b, 1946	Iron Maiden, 1941	War Admiral, 1934	Man o' War Brushup
		Betty Derr, 1928	Sir Gallahad III Uncle's Lassie

SWAPS' RACE RECORD

Swaps ch. c. 1952, by Khaled (Hyperion)–Iron Reward, by Beau Pere
Own.– R.C. Ellsworth
Br.– Rex C. Ellsworth (Cal)
Tr.– M.A. Tenney
Lifetime record: 25 19 2 2 $848,900

3Sep56- 8Was	fst 1	:22^1 :44^1 1:07^4 1:33^2	3↑	Wash Park H 142k	5	3	2^2	$1^{\frac12}$	1^3	1^2	Shoemaker W	130	w	*.40	102-13	Swaps130^{2}Summer Tan115^{2}Sea o Erin112^3	Well in hand late	6
25Aug56- 8Was	fm 1$\frac{3}{16}$Ⓣ	:47 1:10^3 1:36^2 1:55	3↑	Arch Ward Mem H 54k	7	2	$3^{\frac12}$	2^{hd}	3^1	$7^{6\frac14}$	Shoemaker W	130	w	*.30	92-02	Mahan114$^{\frac12}$SirTribal116$^{1\frac34}$PrincMorv113^{hd}	Well up,no excuse	8
25Jly56- 7Hol	fst 1⅝	:46^3 1:36^1 2:00^3 2:38^1	3↑	Sunset H 110k	5	1	$1^{1\frac12}$	$1^{1\frac12}$	1^6	$1^{4\frac14}$	Shoemaker W	130	w	*.10	112-08	Swaps130$^{4\frac14}$Honeys Alibi108^{1}Blue Volt108^3	Eased up late	9
14Jly56- 8Hol	fst 1¼	:45^2 1:09 1:33^1 1:58^3	3↑	Hol Gold Cup H 162k	3	1	2^2	1^{hd}	1^4	1^2	Shoemaker W	130	w	*.15	105-05	Swaps130^{2}MisterGus117$^{1\frac14}$Porterhouse119$^{2\frac14}$	Eased at finish	7
4Jly56- 8Hol	fst 1⅛	:46^2 1:09^2 1:34 1:46^4	3↑	American H 103k	3	3	$3^{4\frac12}$	3^{nk}	1^3	$1^{1\frac34}$	Shoemaker W	130	w	*.20	100-12	Swaps130$^{1\frac34}$MstrGus111^{6}BobbyBrocto115^8	Eased final stages	5
23Jun56- 7Hol	fst 1$\frac{1}{16}$	:23^1 :46 1:09 1:39	3↑	Inglewood H 52k	5	3	$2^{1\frac12}$	1^{hd}	1^3	$1^{2\frac34}$	Shoemaker W	130	w	*.30	107-06	Swaps130$^{2\frac34}$MisterGus115^{2}BobbyBrocto121^7	Eased final 16th	7
9Jun56- 7Hol	fst 1	:22^2 :45^1 1:08^4 1:33^1	3↑	Argonaut H 52k	1	1	1^1	$1^{\frac12}$	1^2	$1^{1\frac14}$	Shoemaker W	128	w	*.20	108-07	Swaps128$^{1\frac14}$Bobby Brocato123^{6}Porterhouse119$^{2\frac34}$	In hand	6
26May56- 7Hol	fst 1$\frac{1}{16}$	:23 :45^3 1:09^2 1:40^4	3↑	Californian 109k	6	4	$2^{1\frac12}$	$1^{\frac12}$	1^3	2^{hd}	Shoemaker W	127	w	*.35	98-11	Porterhse118^{hd}Swaps127^{5}MistrGus118$^{1\frac34}$	Eased by mistake	6
14Apr56- 7GP	fst 1 70	:23 :45^3 1:09^2 1:39^3	3↑	Broward H 25k	4	2	2^2	$1^{1\frac12}$	1^3	$1^{2\frac14}$	Shoemaker W	130	w	*.30	105-09	Swaps130$^{2\frac14}$Gldr105^{5}OurGob114^{no}	Never to a drive,eased up	8
17Feb56- 7SA	fst 1$\frac{1}{16}$	:22^4 :46^2 1:10^3 1:43	4↑	Handicap 15000	7	4	4^2	1^{hd}	1^{hd}	$1^{1\frac34}$	Shoemaker W	127	w	*.70	89-15	Swaps127$^{1\frac34}$Bobby Brocato124^{nk}Arrogate115^9	Strong finish	7
31Aug55- 7Was	gd 1¼	:46 1:10^2 1:37^3 2:04^1		WP Match 100k	2	2	2^1	$2^{1\frac12}$	2^2	$2^{6\frac12}$	Shoemaker W	126	w	*.30	74-17	Nashua126$^{6\frac12}$Swaps126	Wide on stretch turn,tired,swerved	2
20Aug55- 7Was	fm 1$\frac{3}{16}$Ⓣ	:47^2 1:11^4 1:35^4 1:54^3		American Derby 146k	5	1	1^1	$1^{1\frac12}$	1^3	1^1	Shoemaker W	126	w	*.20	101-05	Swaps126^{1}Traffic Judge119^{4}Parador113$^{1\frac12}$	Very handy score	6
9Jly55- 7Hol	fst 1¼	:46^3 1:10^2 1:34^4 2:00^3		Westerner 57k	1	1	$1^{1\frac12}$	1^2	1^{10}	1^6	Shoemaker W	126	w	*.05	96-11	Swaps126^{6}Fabulous Vegas117^{1}Jean's Joe120$^{3\frac12}$	Eased up	5
11Jun55- 7Hol	fst 1$\frac{1}{16}$	:23^1 :46 1:10 1:40^2	3↑	Californian 109k	1	1	2^2	2^1	1^1	$1^{1\frac14}$	Erb D	115	w	*.65	103-06	Swaps115$^{1\frac14}$Detrmine126$^{\frac12}$MistrGus117^3	In hand throughout	6
30May55- 6Hol	fst 1	:22^2 :45^2 1:10^1 1:35		©Will Rogers 27k	3	3	$2^{1\frac12}$	1^{hd}	1^3	1^{12}	Shoemaker W	126	w	*.15e	100-07	Swaps126^{12}Bequeath122^{no}Mr.Sullivan118^3	Drew out in hand	6
7May55- 7CD	fst 1¼	:47^2 1:12^2 1:37 2:01^4		Ky Derby 152k	8	1	1^1	$1^{\frac12}$	$1^{\frac12}$	$1^{1\frac12}$	Shoemaker W	126	w	2.80	98-12	Swps126$^{1\frac12}$Nshua126$^{6\frac12}$SummrTn126^4	Drew clear when urged	10
30Apr55- 6CD	fst 6f	:23 :46^2 1:10^1		Alw 5000	1	3	$1^{2\frac12}$	1^2	1^4	$1^{8\frac12}$	Shoemaker W	123	w	*.30	99-13	Swaps123$^{8\frac12}$TrimDestiny115$^{\frac34}$Styrunnr110$^{4\frac12}$	Speed in reserve	5
19Feb55- 7SA	fst 1⅛	:45^4 1:10^3 1:37 1:50		SA Derby 137k	12	3	3^1	1^3	1^1	$1^{\frac12}$	Longden J	118	w	3.60e	91-14	Swaps118$^{\frac12}$Jean'sJoe118$^{3\frac12}$BlueRuler118^3	Went wide,driving	14
19Jan55- 7SA	my 7f	:21^4 :45 1:10^3 1:24		San Vicente 22k	1	5	$5^{6\frac12}$	2^1	1^2	$1^{3\frac12}$	Shoemaker W	116	w	4.40e	83-25	Swaps116$^{3\frac12}$Trentonian120^{hd}Jean'sJoe114^6	Speed in reserve	8
30Dec54- 6SA	fst 6f	:22^1 :45^1 1:10		Alw 6000	5	5	2^{hd}	2^1	2^{hd}	1no	Shoemaker W	118	w	5.25	95-11	Swaps118^{no}Beau Busher113$^{1\frac34}$Battle Dance118$^{\frac12}$	Strong drive	12
8Jly54- 6Hol	fst 5½f	:22^1 :45^3 :58^1 1:04^4		©CS Howard 29k	1	5	$6^{3\frac12}$	$6^{5\frac14}$	5^8	$5^{8\frac34}$	Burton J	118	w	9.95e	85-12	ColonlMack114$^{\frac34}$Mr.Sullivan122^{1}BackHo118^1	Showed nothing	6
22Jun54- 7Hol	fst 5f	:22^1 :45^4 :58^2		©Haggin 24k	9	7	$8^{3\frac34}$	7^3	$3^{1\frac12}$	3^2	Burton J	122	w	6.40e	92-13	Mr. Sullivan114$^{\frac12}$Back Hoe122$^{1\frac12}$Swaps122$^{1\frac34}$	Good effort	10
10Jun54- 7Hol	fst 5f	:22^1 :46 :58^2		©June Juv 16k	5	5	$4^{2\frac12}$	3^2	$1^{\frac12}$	$1^{2\frac12}$	Burton J	116	w	4.70	94-10	Swaps116$^{2\frac12}$Trentonian119^{2}Noir116^{nk}	Drew out	7
3Jun54- 7Hol	fst 5f	:22^1 :45^2 :58		Westchester 16k	2	5	$4^{2\frac12}$	$5^{3\frac12}$	$5^{1\frac34}$	$3^{2\frac14}$	Burton J	116	w	7.25	94-11	Back Hoe119$^{1\frac14}$Trentcnian119^{1}Swaps116$^{\frac12}$	Failed to rally	7
20May54- 2Hol	fst 5f	:22^2 :45^4 :58^2		©Md Sp Wt	9	5	2^{hd}	2^{hd}	1^{hd}	1^3	Burton J	120	w	12.60	94-12	Swaps120^{3}Irish Cheer120$^{3\frac12}$Battle Dance120$^{1\frac12}$	Won handily	11

Index

Photo Credits

Cover photo: (The Blood-Horse)

Page 1: Swaps winning the American (The Blood-Horse); Swaps head shot (The Blood-Horse)

Page 2: Hyperion (The Blood-Horse); Khaled (Bob Hopper); Iron Reward (Giles E. Wright); Beau Pere (The Blood-Horse)

Page 3: Rex Ellsworth and Mesach Tenney (CTBA); Swaps feeding at Ellsworth ranch (The Blood-Horse)

Page 4: Swaps as a two-year-old (Hollywood Park); Swaps winning the San Vicente (CTBA); Tenney shoeing Swaps (Giles E. Wright)

Page 5: Swaps winning the Santa Anita Derby; In the Santa Anita Derby winner's circle (both The Blood-Horse)

Page 6: Swaps walking the Churchill Downs backside (The Blood-Horse); Kentucky Derby win (Bernie Metzroth); Wearing the roses (Louisville Courier-Journal)

Page 7: Getting off the train (CTBA); Grooms working on Swaps' hoof (Hollywood Park); In the Will Rogers Stakes winner's circle (The Blood-Horse)

Page 8: Winning the Californian; Winning the Westerner (both The Blood-Horse)

Page 9: Winning the American Derby (The Blood-Horse); Swaps-Nashua match race (Keeneland-Morgan)

Page 10: Swaps resting (Giles E. Wright); Discussing Swaps' foot (Doug Wilson)

Page 11: Winning the overnight handicap; Winning the Broward (both The Blood-Horse)

Page 12: In the American Handicap winner's circle; Winning the Hollywood Gold Cup (both The Blood-Horse)

Page 13: Winning the Sunset Handicap (The Blood-Horse); Swaps and groom Josie Kascendi (Hollywood Park)

Page 14: Swaps at Darby Dan Farm (The Blood-Horse); John and Dorothy Galbreath (Dell Hancock)

Page 15: Affectionately (Mike Sirico/NYRA); Chateaugay (The Blood-Horse); Primonetta (Turfotos)

Page 16: Swaps' gravestone (Tracy Gantz); Swaps statue at Hollywood Park (Shigeki Kikkawa)

ABOUT THE
AUTHOR

Barry Irwin, who began his career as a Turf writer, is best known today as president of Team Valor racing stable.

The California native has written for *The Blood-Horse, Thoroughbred of California,* and *Daily Racing Form.* He also served as U.S. correspondent for the *New Zealand Breeders' Bulletin,* Southern California reporter for *The Thoroughbred Record,* and freelance contributor to numerous other publications. In addition, Irwin has scripted film projects and hosted radio and television programs.

Since the late 1980s, Irwin has formed racing partnerships, first under the *nom de course* of Clover Racing Stables and since 1992 as head of Team Valor. Grade I winners prospected, syndicated, and managed by Irwin include Prized (Breeders' Cup Turf), Star of Cozzene (Arlington Million), and Captain Bodgit (Florida Derby).

Irwin and his wife, Elizabeth (Becky) Raine Irwin, live in Versailles, Kentucky, with their daughter, Chloe Alys Irwin.

Forthcoming titles
in the

THOROUGHBRED
Legends®

series:

Affirmed and Alydar

Round Table

War Admiral

Exterminator

Carry Back

Available titles

Man o' War

Dr. Fager

Citation

Go for Wand

Seattle Slew

Forego

Native Dancer

Nashua

Spectacular Bid

John Henry

Personal Ensign

Sunday Silence

Ruffian

www.thoroughbredlegends.com